WOUNDED EAGLE

The Game Beyond the Foul Poles

by

J. Terry Johnson

Copyright © 2013 by J. Terry Johnson

Wounded Eagle
The Game Beyond the Foul Poles
by J. Terry Johnson

Printed in the United States of America

ISBN 9781626979987

1. Literature & Fiction: Genre Fiction: Sports
2. Sports & Outdoors: Baseball
3. Religion & Spirituality: Christianity: Christian Living: Faith

All rights reserved solely by the author. The author guarantees all contents are original and do not infringe upon the legal rights of any other person or work. No part of this publication may be reproduced, stored in a retrieval system or transmitted in any way by any means, electronic, mechanical, photocopy, recording or otherwise without the prior permission of the the author except as provided by USA copyright law. The views expressed in this book are not necessarily those of the publisher.

Unless otherwise indicated, Bible quotations are taken from the New King James Version. Copyright © 1982 by Thomas Nelson, Inc.

www.xulonpress.com

Dedication

Wounded Eagle is dedicated to my brothers, Tim and Stan Johnson, who share my enthusiasm for the game of baseball. Tim is an avid Los Angeles Angel fan, while Stan and I root passionately for the St. Louis Cardinals. When conversations regarding current events and our family circle have run their courses, we can always talk about baseball.

Acknowledgments

Some debts are more difficult to repay than others. By the time we reach adulthood, there are any number of teachers, coaches, and preachers to acknowledge as mentors who have had an influence in shaping our lives. I have such a list. Most of those people are now deceased. Some I visited before their passing and expressed my personal gratitude; for others, I was too late.

A name that never appeared on my "mentors list"—but should have—was John R. Tunis. We never met in person; he never knew my name. But as an elementary school kid growing up in the early 1950s, I was the perfect age to be reading juvenile fiction written by John R. Tunis (1889-1975).

On Saturday mornings, when I made a weekly trip to the local library, I often looked for his name on book spines, hoping to find a new title I hadn't read. Tunis wrote about baseball players, and in those days my whole world was centered on baseball. He wrote about the "Kid," "Highpockets," and Bones Hathaway, the sensational rookie pitcher who helped the Dodgers win a pennant. Had my teachers not insisted I write my book reports on literary classics, I might never have graduated from John R. Tunis and his juvenile fiction. *Wounded Eagle* is my contribution to his genre.

Inspiration strikes in some unusual settings. The storyline for *Wounded Eagle* came to me, of all places, while sailing upon the high seas. My wife and I were with our children and grandchildren aboard one of the largest cruise ships in the world when the outline for this book popped into my head. Although being careful to enjoy this memorable vacation experience with the family, I stole a few moments for myself that week to fantasize what might occur if a new Major League Baseball franchise were awarded to San Antonio, the nation's seventh-largest city and a metropolitan area located within eighty miles of our home in the Texas Hill Country. Voilà!

Words cannot adequately express my gratitude to Nolan Ryan for consenting to write the foreword to *Wounded Eagle*. No Major League Baseball player, whether currently on a team roster or retired from the game, commands more respect from the fans in the state of Texas than Nolan Ryan. His career stats are

Acknowledgments

incredible. Twenty-seven years pitching in the Major Leagues. The winning pitcher on 324 occasions. An amazing record of 5,714 strikeouts! An unbelievable seven no-hitters! Eight times selected to the Major League Baseball All-Star Game! And the ultimate triumph of any professional player, induction into Baseball's Hall of Fame in Cooperstown in 1999.

But his outstanding career on the playing field only tells part of the story about Nolan Ryan and the legend he has become. He is a devoted husband, father, and grandfather. We both have grandchildren in the same Christian school in Austin and I have personally seen him humbled by the open expression of love and respect coming from his family.

A special "thanks" also to Reid Ryan and his business associate Sherry Clawson for making the appeal to Reid's father on my behalf. I am both grateful and honored by his acceptance.

Finally, I extend a "shout out" to Kylie Lyons for her editorial assistance and to the professional staff at Xulon Press for extending me excellent layout, cover design, and marketing services. This book has been an amazing team effort. I hope that you, the readers, enjoy the finished product as much as I have enjoyed writing it.

Contents

Foreword xii

1. The Press Conference 17
2. Looking Back 26
3. The Trade that Made a Difference 34
4. First Impressions 41
5. Caught in the Middle 49
6. Rookie Romance 57
7. Taking the Plunge 65
8. A Bad Day at Wrigley 74
9. A Secret Exposed 83
10. A Stranger at the Door 91
11. An Unforgettable Ceremony 100
12. Trouble in Paradise 108
13. Digging Deep for Answers 116
14. A Championship Season 123
15. Killing Daddy 131
16. Hiring a New Manager 139
17. Unsettled Business 148

Foreword

There is nothing quite like a good baseball story. You know the type. Most readers anticipate the ending well before the last chapter. With the exception of that fellow named "Casey" who played in Mudville, the hero is always at bat in the bottom of the ninth representing the winning run, and then smashes a homerun that sails well beyond the outfield fence. Having been a pitcher, I always grimace when I read about the "crack of the bat" and the fans "craning their necks" to see where the baseball landed. About that time I usually close the book and head for the shower.

Wounded Eagle is a baseball story of a different kind. It does have some dramatic baseball scenes that occur on the diamond, but the story is more about the ballplayers and their lives outside the ballpark. The book focuses on the relationships that impact the players' performances on the field and the emotional makeup that often defines who these gifted athletes really are.

From my own personal experience, I can tell you that there are some interesting characters who have become Major League Baseball players. Most of them are good guys, wanting to do the right thing, and they are a joy to have as teammates. But, as in any occupation, there are always a few exceptions. *Wounded Eagle* is an account of a young man who is a superstar on the baseball field, but encounters considerable difficulty in handling the trials of everyday life.

Unless you have spent years playing the game at the professional level, you cannot imagine the challenges that these athletes face in bringing their lives into balance. Extensive road trips disrupt normal family life, resulting in added stress for husbands, wives, and their young children. And unbridled fan adulation can do a number on the best of men. It can be difficult to leave those issues at the doorstep when the professional returns home at night.

Spend a few hours with Randy Dobson, Bill Simons and their teammates, playing for Major League Baseball's newly awarded franchise team in

San Antonio – the Eagles. *Wounded Eagle* will take you well beyond the foul poles.

Nolan Ryan

Chapter 1

The Press Conference

"Every way of a man is right in his own eyes, but the Lord weighs the hearts."
Proverbs 21:2

For the last time in his long, distinguished career, Randy Dobson stood before the media as field manager of the San Antonio Eagles. An assortment of local and national sportswriters were packed into Gainsworth Stadium's pressroom, taking careful notes as Dobson announced his decision to resign a post he had held for more than twenty years. The decision to walk away had not come easily; it was, in fact, one he had been pondering for months.

The Eagles' public relations staff had been one of the first in Major League Baseball to employ an interactive television conferencing system, enabling baseball writers and media outlets to cover the team's press meetings from all parts of the globe. It featured the latest advancements in communications technology and was the pride of the club's front office. Fifty-three off-site correspondents had opted to participate in today's special event via long distance.

"Why have you chosen to retire now, Randy?" asked *Sporting News* reporter Neil Cummings, who was linked to the interactive system from his e-publication's headquarters in New York. He appeared via satellite on the ten-foot wide screen immediately left of the rostrum on the front wall of the pressroom. "Have you received any pressure from the front office?"

"No, the decision was mine," Dobson said, a bit too defiantly. The veteran manager was miffed that anyone would give thought to such a question, let alone ask it at a national press conference. He knew the drill: Every writer wanted to develop a unique storyline to make his column stand out from others. Unfortunately, a few of the reporters chased cats down blind alleys when the facts would not support them, and Randy had been burnt by Cummings once or twice before.

"I've always been impressed with Tony La Russa's philosophy on management, including his preference for signing one-year contracts. He never wanted to be obligated to the Cardinals or any other club on a long-term contract, just hanging on to his job when the fire inside him had burned out; neither do I. I've run out of gas. It's time for someone new, someone fresh to take the reins. The Eagle players deserve that, and so do their fans."

Randy had always been a fan favorite in San Antonio. Now fifty-three years old, the six-foot-tall sandy-headed icon had spent ten years as a player in Major League Baseball and twice that many as a manager, all with the San Antonio Eagles. From the first time he had picked up a hollow plastic bat and swung it as a three-year-old, Randy had been in love with the game. Baseball was his passion, or, as his wife, Becky, often said, "Baseball is Randy's mistress."

"What are your plans for next year? And the years after that?" Butch Lemery, long-time writer for the *San Antonio Express-News*, asked. The third-largest daily newspaper in Texas commanded extra respect from all the Eagle players and coaches. Each morning's issue ran at least two, sometimes as many as four or five articles about the Eagles. With the stroke of a computer keyboard the local sportswriters assigned to cover the team could make or break a ballplayer's reputation with the fans. During Randy's tenure with the Eagles, the *Express-News* had been generous to him, and he chose his words carefully.

"The Eagles and I have had some discussion about that, but I have nothing to report at this time," Randy said, pausing to wipe away a maverick tear that had formed in the corner of his left eye. He knew a contract calling for him to work in the front office was soon to be tendered, but he and Becky would need some time to think through the ramifications of launching a new phase of his baseball career.

The game had been good to Randy over the years, and he had been wise in managing his retirement investments, amassing more equities than he could have imagined when he'd finished his collegiate baseball career at Arizona State. If he and Becky chose to leave baseball entirely, they would not have to worry about finances. His main concern was for the Eagles; did he still have anything to offer them in a front office position?

Randy had been advised to put some distance between himself and the Eagles, lest his shadow fall heavily upon his successor, a person yet to be named. New managers were ticklish on the subject. Their predecessors were sometimes perceived as rivals in the clubhouse, vying for the players' deeper loyalty and respect. Randy understood the sticking point, but he had invested so much of himself in the Eagle franchise that he hated to leave the organization if there were a productive role he could play in its future. He set the matter aside for today; it would have to be settled later.

"Have you heard any speculation about your successor?" Ancil Reeves, ESPN's top baseball analyst from Atlanta, appeared on the pressroom's large screen. Several faces flashed through Randy's mind, but it was too soon to speculate, and, besides, it was not his call.

"Ask me that question a month from now, Ancil." Randy chuckled. "Your guess is as good as mine."

Truthfully, Randy had given considerable thought to the question. Now was the time for the Eagles to make a bold move: go with a younger man. Randy had been thirty-one years old when he became San Antonio's second field boss. The experiment of hiring a popular former player, youthful but driven to succeed in every facet of the game, had proven to be a wise choice then, and he saw no reason why it should be any different now.

For decades San Antonio had been known as a basketball mecca. The Spurs had been a dominant force in the National Basketball Association, having won the NBA championship four times between 1999 and 2007, and on two more recent occasions in 2020 and 2022. The nation's seventh-largest city was still without a National Football League franchise, but in late 2013 Major League Baseball had made San Antonio one of its four expansion cities, bringing the Lone Star State its third Major League team.

The public relations firm of Thomas, Turnbow, and Gonzales had been retained to find the perfect nickname for the new team. A fan contest was launched, and San Antonians submitted their favorites, while the firm utilized a computer software program to generate hundreds of additional names appropriate for the region. Burros, Coyotes, and Bucks appeared to be the most popular names recommended by fans.

A massive write-in campaign from current and former military families made a solid case for the "San Antonio Eagles," and the matter was quickly resolved. The city had enjoyed a long-standing affiliation with the United States military; major bases located in the region had added jobs and economic stability to South Central Texas for many years. What better way to pay homage to all who had worn the nation's colors than to use the eagle—the well-known symbol of freedom and strength—as the team's nickname? Case closed. Uniforms were quickly designed,

The Press Conference

featuring Texas bluebonnet blue, white, and silver. Each jersey proudly displayed script-lettering across the chest: *Eagles*.

Along with San Antonio, New Orleans was awarded a new franchise, and MLB's National League was reconfigured. Instead of three divisions, there were now four, each comprised of five teams. The Eagles, along with the Houston Astros, the Atlanta Braves, the Florida Marlins, and the New Orleans Gators, competed in the NL South.

After the completion of major revisions to Nelson Wolff Municipal Stadium, former home of the Texas League's San Antonio Missions, the Eagles began the 2015 season with a capacity crowd of 32,216 fans attending Opening Day. The renovated stadium had been renamed Eagle Park and was commonly referred to by locals as "The Nest." Although fielding a losing team, the Eagles continued to draw large crowds, competing favorably for the summer-entertainment dollars with Fiesta Texas, SeaWorld, the Alamo, and the city's internationally acclaimed River Walk. From its inception, Major League Baseball was a big hit in South Central Texas.

After playing eight years in the small confines of Eagle Park, the team moved into an amazing new baseball stadium located on the grounds of the 1968

HemisFair. Franchise owners, working with city officials and corporate leaders, constructed a futuristic stadium unlike anything ever seen in the Major Leagues. The project became viable only when the city received a major grant from local philanthropist and oilman Eugene Lester Gainsworth, and within weeks the city's mayor announced that the new edifice would bear the donor's name: Gainsworth Stadium.

After several minutes of fielding questions, Randy was ready for the press conference to be over. Knowing that his words could be misconstrued or bent to fit a reporter's personal bias, he had never been fully at ease with the media. Today was no exception. Beads of sweat formed along his receding hairline, and he reached for a handkerchief in his back pocket to wipe away the perspiration.

"Last question," Herman Flannery, Eagles Vice President for Press Relations, announced.

"What will it take to get the Eagles back in the World Series?" Nick Hammond, chief baseball reporter for *Sports Illustrated*, asked the bell ringer. The Eagles had won two World Series Championships under Randy, but the team had not been in contention three of the last four years. Nick had made the trip from New York to San Antonio to cover the news event and had asked for some private time with

Randy following the press conference or first thing in the morning.

"Let me think about that one overnight, Nick. I'll share my thoughts with you tomorrow at breakfast," Randy said, dodging a question that would have taken hours to discuss in a meaningful way.

"Thanks to all of you for coming today, but, more importantly, thanks for all you have done to advance my career over the years," Randy said. He stepped away from the microphone to a smattering of applause from the reporters and media crews. A chapter was closing in his life, and the future was anyone's guess. Whatever was to come would have to wait until tomorrow.

Chapter 2

Looking Back

"A man's heart plans his way, but the Lord directs his steps."

Proverbs 16:9

Three years ago, Randy and Becky had sold their fashionable home in Alamo Heights and moved into a new resort community north of San Antonio, just three miles south of Boerne. They made their home in the Texas Hill Country, surrounded by a menagerie of wildlife and plants displaying a brilliant array of beautiful colors. Nothing was more inspiring to Randy than traveling the back roads, winding through the rolling hills in the springtime when the native wildflowers put on their annual show.

Whatever he chose to do with the Eagles, Randy had found the place where he wanted to spend the rest of his life.

At the beckoning of a 6:00 a.m. alarm, Randy crawled out of bed. After a quick shower, he dressed in khaki slacks and a blue button-down Oxford shirt and kissed Becky goodbye.

"I'll be home before noon," he said as he opened the door leading into the garage. His latest rage, a high-performance electric car, awaited him: a two-door cherry red Pegasus 500 convertible, the current generation's equivalent of a 1960's vintage Corvette. Becky had accused him of going through a midlife crisis when he had brought it home last month.

"Next it'll be gold chains," she'd teased. Maybe she was right about a midlife crisis, but there would be no gold chains around his neck; he was sure of that.

The sleek sports car was more powerful than any gas model Randy had ever owned. It was capable of reaching speeds greater than 150 miles per hour on Super Highways, new high-tech autobahns recently built to link major cities throughout Texas. Although he was running a few minutes late for his breakfast appointment with Nick Hammond, Randy wouldn't need to crank the Pegasus up nearly that fast this morning.

The relentless heat of an Indian summer in South Central Texas was oppressive, even in the early morning hours. No rain had fallen over the last six weeks, and now, in October, the high temperatures were still hovering near one hundred degrees. Randy decided to leave the car's top up and blast the air conditioner as high as it would go.

Nick had suggested they meet for breakfast at Callahan's, an overrated steak house, located on U.S. Highway 281, two miles north of Loop 1604. Randy knew how to get to the restaurant, but he had never considered it a great place to have breakfast.

Maybe Nick wants a place where we won't be interrupted, he mused as he sped southeast toward his destination. Saturday morning traffic was lighter than the weekday commuter assault that often turned the eight-lane freeway into a parking lot.

Randy's car phone chimed. He touched a button on the steering wheel. Upon connection, a picture of Nick Hammond appeared on the Pegasus's GPS screen.

"Good morning, Nick," Randy said as he exited the freeway. "Are you already at Callahan's?"

"I've been waiting fifteen minutes. Thought you might have overslept, maybe stood me up."

"I'm pulling into the parking lot as we speak," Randy said, assuring his host.

Nick Hammond was a legend in the Baseball Writers' Association of America. He had covered every Major League All-Star Game and World Series since 1996, and he had cast a ballot each year for a few of those who were fortunate enough to have been nominated for enshrinement into the National Baseball Hall of Fame in Cooperstown, New York. This was not the first time he had asked for an interview with Randy, and although the Eagle manager had grimaced when reading his own words in Hammond's previous articles, he appreciated that Nick had always portrayed him fairly in the pages of *Sports Illustrated*.

Randy spotted Nick in a corner booth. He was stirring a cup of cream-laced coffee and tinkering with his recorder. As Randy approached, Nick picked up a note pad of scribbling, likely notes taken at yesterday's press conference, and moved it to the far end of the table. The two men shook hands just before Randy slipped into his side of the booth.

"How did you know about Callahan's?" Randy asked. "Aren't you staying somewhere downtown? It's not close."

"Laird and I used to meet here," Nick said. "He liked it here. Less likelihood of being interrupted by the autograph hounds."

Randy understood all too well and smiled, his memory flooded with visions of Laird.

Wilson "Pop" Laird managed the Eagles when they began their inaugural season in 2015. He was a large man who hailed from South Georgia and spoke with a noticeable southern drawl. After his Major League playing days were over, he began coaching in the minor leagues. The Braves brought him to Atlanta as their bench coach, giving him the opportunity to circulate once again at the Major League level.

Wilson's brother, Walton Laird, was general manager of the Los Angeles Dodgers. He had been instrumental in getting Wilson his initial interview with the Eagles and did what he could from a distance to help Wilson land the job. Both men were "lifers" when it came to baseball.

A bleach-blonde waitress in her late forties approached the booth, fumbling with a pencil, an order pad, and a couple of grease-stained menus, which she offered with no smile and minimal eye contact. "What'll it be this morning?" she asked, her voice husky like that of a smoker.

"Make mine *huevos rancheros* and a little more coffee and cream," Nick said without a peek at his menu. "I can't get good Mexican food back home." He smiled, looking up at the waitress, as if he needed to explain his quick response. "Every time I come to Texas, I make sure to get my fill."

"I'll have the same," Randy said, "but make my coffee black." The woman scribbled the orders onto the pad and scurried away toward the kitchen.

"What did you learn from Laird?" Nick asked.

"Just about everything," Randy said, as though confessing. "He was a tough, old-school, play-by-the-rules sort, but he treated his players with respect. I thought of him as a southern gentleman in baseball cleats.

"He had a great eye for talent. He put together a coaching staff that was second to none in my book. When I took the reins from Pop, I stepped into a manager's dream. He had already assembled the core of my staff; all I had to do was supply the spark and the willpower to take the organization to the next level. I'll always stand on Pop's shoulders."

Laird had never won a pennant in his twelve years as manager in San Antonio. Had the Eagles not been an expansion club—where little was expected in the early years—he would have lost his job after three or four seasons. As it turned out, the Eagles finished in the cellar his first two years and did not have a winning season until Randy was called up as a rookie infielder from the Triple-A affiliate in Austin. From that year forward Laird never had a losing season, but he didn't win any National League pennants, not even a division title.

"One thing that always impressed me about Laird was how he was able to work with the Latinos," Nick said, taking a sip of his fresh cup of coffee. "You would have thought an ol' Georgia boy would've been a real redneck, but the Hispanics seemed to love him. What do you make of that?"

No doubt about it, the Eagles had more than their share of Hispanics on the roster. Randy had always thought being in San Antonio helped, but Nick was right: Laird had fostered a climate that made Caribbean-born athletes along with players from Central and South America feel right at home in the big leagues. He and the front office had even managed to bring Puerto Rican Yadier Molina—or Yadi, as he had been known as a young catcher for the St. Louis Cardinals—to the Eagles in 2018, when the aging superstar opted to try his hand at free agency.

"Laird was intuitive, had people skills," Randy said. "And he was a credit to the game. I only wish we could have won a pennant, a division title, something significant before he hung up his spikes."

"That brings me to why I asked you here, Randy," Nick said. "Was yesterday's announcement the script for how you envisioned your managerial career ending?"

"I could have wished that press conference had been held immediately after the Eagles had won the World Series, if that's what you mean," Randy said. "It never feels good to step out of the limelight when you're not playing at your best, but that's how it seems to work in this business. Not too many of us get to do what La Russa did, end a storybook managerial career one week after winning a third World Series. I don't have any regrets. I had the privilege of managing one Major League Baseball team for twenty-one years and brought home two World Series rings during that run. I can live with that record during my retirement years."

"Take me back to the day you became the Eagles' manager," Nick said. "Do you mind if I turn on the recorder?"

Chapter 3

The Trade that Made a Difference

"He who walks with integrity walks securely, but he who perverts his ways will become known."

Proverbs 10:9

Randy was silent for a few moments, reflecting upon Nick's question, a flood of events that had occurred during his first year as field manager of the San Antonio Eagles projecting on a screen inside his mind. The formal announcement of his appointment was a red-letter day, a mountaintop experience as thrilling right at this moment as it was more than two decades ago. He was young, inexperienced, and unafraid of the future. If he'd known then what he knew today about managing a Major League Baseball team, he would have stood shaking in his cleats.

"I was too young to understand what was being asked of me," Randy said. "Pop had been suffering from chest pains, and the doctor told him he needed rest. The stars aligned. Looking back, I can hardly believe the club's ownership turned in my direction."

"Did they interview other candidates?"

"They did. Skip Reynolds was the hitting coach in Cincinnati then. He had ten years of piloting a team in Triple-A and considerably more wins than losses. I thought for sure he'd get the job. His family didn't want to live in Texas, so at the last minute he withdrew his name from consideration."

"And then they came to you?"

"Well, not exactly. I knew my playing days were over. After breaking my ankle early in the season, my speed diminished. I lost some of my range around second base. It was time to hang it up.

"When I told Pop about my decision, he said to keep it under wraps. He had an idea. He'd had sessions with his doctors and knew it was his last season at the helm. I think he wanted to buy some time to convince the owners and front office to take a chance on me as his successor. His persistence coaxed the suits to come knocking on my door."

"How did the first year go?" Nick asked, one eyebrow raised, eyes scanning Randy's body language for the slightest reaction.

"The fans were great," Randy said, a warm smile brightening his face. "I always enjoyed the fans. They were extremely generous in their support of me—even the first year when we struggled to stay above .500. I can't say the same about a couple of the owners."

"You had trouble pleasing the owners?"

"Two of the more influential owners were convinced I was too young and inexperienced to handle the job," Randy said. "They adored Pop, thought he walked on water. Toward the end of the season I began to think my tenure was heading for an abrupt end. That summer odds were not favorable that I could survive two years as manager, let alone twenty."

Randy spent the next few minutes recounting some of the more enjoyable memories from his first year as the Eagles' new skipper: Opening Day ceremonies with Wilson Laird handing the line-up card to Randy at home plate; sweeping the Dodgers, the defending World Champions, just before the All-Star break; and the no-hitter, tossed by the club's ace, Miles Daniels, at Gainsworth Stadium in late September. Each moment had provided Randy with the burst of energy he needed to deal with the enormous task that had become his livelihood.

"I couldn't have made it through that first year had it not been for Pop and the coaching staff that he left." Randy sipped lukewarm coffee. "We were on the cusp of doing something great in San Antonio. To a man, the coaches' confidence in our future fueled my own. We worked well together, had great chemistry and genuine respect for the talents of one another."

Laird had assembled a talented staff of mentors, led by his pitching coach, Roy S. Westbrooke. Only twelve years older than Randy, Roy had coached at some level of professional baseball for more than twenty years and was the consummate team player. Regardless of his senior experience, he had unwavering respect for the chain of command.

Randy believed Roy could get more out of a pitching staff than any coach in the game. Some thought Roy to be excessively opinionated, but Randy found strength in his coach's ability to work through knotty issues, weigh the facts, and come to a sensible decision. Far more often than not, Roy's judgment was sound and unassailable.

The hitting coach, Gabby Rhodes, turned out to be Randy's closest confidant. Only one year older than Randy, Gabby was quite a character on the bench. When the team was on the road, Randy and Gabby were inseparable, occasionally causing petty jealousies to arise among other coaches or players. Randy gave little attention to those concerns. Gabby was the one person who could make him laugh, even after the Eagles had been shut out or routed by their opponents.

Randy suspected Nick had probably had enough of strolling down memory lane, but one pivotal event that had occurred during the first year had not been mentioned: the late-season trade for Bill Simons.

"Enough with that, though," Randy said. "Nick, do you remember the trade we made in the fall of '27?" Randy asked. The memory was fresh in his mind, as though it had happened yesterday.

"Vaguely," Nick said.

"It may have been the most important trade we made in the first thirteen years of the franchise. Getting Molina was ground-shaking at the time, but it didn't change the dynamic of our club as much as acquiring Bill Simons from the Royals' farm system. Raymond Smithwick, Director of Player Development, had been watching Simons pitch for Omaha every time they played in Austin. He couldn't say enough good things about the kid and insisted we find a way to make room for him on our roster in 2028."

"What did you have to give up in the trade?" Nick asked.

"That's the thing, Nick." Randy smiled. "The Royals were loaded with talent in Kansas City that year and had more starting pitchers than they could possibly use. We got Simons for one minor league infielder and a second-round draft pick. Smithwick's read on the kid turned out to be spot on."

"Any chance Simons might want your job?" Hammonds asked meekly, uncertain as to the response he might receive. Bill Simons was in his third year of managing San Antonio's farm team in Austin, and it had been rumored that he was interested in replacing Dobson.

"It's anyone's guess," Randy said, sidestepping. "He has plenty of support, but he has a host of detractors as well. I guess we'll see before long." Randy took a long pause, mulling over the difficult decision facing the owners and their front office.

"Listen, I need to go. Promised Becky I would be home before noon. Can't believe we've been sitting here four hours."

"Fair enough," Nick said. "You've given me plenty of material for an article."

The two men stood, shook hands, and promised to get together again after the dust had settled.

Randy climbed into his Pegasus 500 and, top down, headed north on U.S. Highway 281, taking the long route home.

Chapter 4

First Impressions

> "As iron sharpens iron, so a man sharpens the countenance of his friend."
>
> Proverbs 27:17

As Randy steered his beloved Pegasus 500 through San Antonio's suburban traffic, then speeding northwest toward the hills surrounding Bourne, he reminisced about his first encounter with Bill Simons. The young manager knew Simons was an exceptional athlete from the moment they'd met. Raymond Smithwick had brokered the introduction, bringing Simons into Randy's office only two days after the trade had been finalized. There he stood: six feet four inches tall and 195 pounds of pure muscle.

What was there not to like? Randy recalled musing to himself at the time.

Simons had grown up in Southwest Kansas, graduating from Liberal High School at the head of his class. After two years at Wichita State University, where he pitched the Shockers baseball team into the quarterfinals of the Collegiate World Series in Omaha, Simons had opted to leave college and enter the Major League Baseball draft. The Kansas City Royals had selected him on their second round and signed him to a minor league contract within three weeks of the day he was drafted.

Simons was sent to Idaho Falls to play rookie league ball that first summer, but the next spring he began his first full season in professional baseball with the Northwest Arkansas Naturals, Kansas City's Double-A affiliate. One year later he was invited to the Royals' spring training camp and was impressive in all three of the games he started; however, a few days prior to the season's opener, Simons was optioned to Omaha, the Royals' Triple-A affiliate, to prove he was ready for the big leagues.

Randy had read some of the newspaper clippings about Simons' season in Omaha. He liked most of what he had read regarding his performance on the pitching mound; it was the reports pertaining to the young hurler's activities away from the ballpark that gave him pause. Overall, he had come to believe that Simons was a good match for what the Eagles needed: a young, durable starting pitcher.

Randy recalled meeting with Simons later that same week at a San Antonio bistro.

"Sorry to be running late, sir," Simons said, *folding his large frame into the café's undersized, tightly spaced booth. "Hope you haven't been waiting long. I had to take my mom on a tour of the Alamo, and we got a little tied up in downtown traffic."*

"No problem," Randy said. "Where does your mother live?"

"She still lives in Kansas," Simons said. "You couldn't move her from Liberal with a herd of elephants."

Randy was touched by the way Simons spoke kindly of his mother. He enjoyed seeing younger players show respect for their elders, whether speaking of family, strangers, or members of his own coaching staff. A kid who knew how to show deference to his elders was someone who would take instruction well. After all, that was Randy's job: to teach young players how to play the game of baseball at the Major League level. If a kid didn't listen to his coaches, he wouldn't last long in the big leagues.

As Randy continued along the South Texas roads, his mind slipped further into that first conversation with Simons.

"So, tell me about your summer in Omaha."

"It was a good growth experience for me, sir," Simons said. *"I finished the year better than I started. April and May were cold months in Omaha, and I never felt my arm was in ideal condition until the middle of June. After that, I won eight games in a row and finished the season with twelve wins and six losses. ERA was 3.12."*

"That's a good year," Randy said, genuinely intending the compliment. *"What about your encounter with the Potter kid?"*

The report was that Simons and Aaron Potter, an outfielder in his seventh year at the AAA level, had been involved in a verbal brawl in the locker room after one of Simons' six losses. Tempers had escalated, and one or two punches had been thrown before the ruckus was brought under control. Both players had been fined by the Omaha front office.

"Ugh," the young man muttered quietly, his countenance wilting. Simons slowly raised his head and looked Randy in the eye. *"That was not my best hour, sir,"* he said, displaying plausible humility. *"Potter told a lie about me to one of our teammates.*

I couldn't let him say those things without standing up for myself. One thing led to another, and before I knew what was happening, he threw a punch."

At that time, Randy remembered feeling that Simons probably had been the victim of an older player's verbal abuse after the rookie's rough outing on the mound. Veteran players loved to take the starch out of their younger teammates.

Of course Simons should have stood up for himself. I would have done the same myself! he'd thought, reading the account in the newspaper so many years before. After years of managing Simons in the Majors, Randy was slightly more sympathetic to what might have been "the rest of the story."

As though on autopilot, Randy pulled into his driveway, opening the garage door from his remote, and drove the Pegasus 500 into its familiar stall within the oversized garage. Although he and Becky were enjoying an empty nest, he still had four automobiles to manage. He couldn't do without his sports car or his Ford pickup, and Becky wouldn't sell her metallic red Lexus sedan or the couple's Lincoln SUV. Their marriage had survived on compromises over the years, but settling on which of two cars to drive had resulted in a marital standoff.

As he walked into the house, he sighed; Becky was waiting for Randy in the kitchen. She was as lovely as the day the two had met, and their love had grown stronger with each passing year. Regardless of whatever scrapes, defeats, and disappointments Randy may have encountered on the baseball field, Becky was his number-one fan. She believed in his goodness and in his judgment to do the right thing. Her smile always turned rainy days into sunshine.

"How did it go with Nick?"

"We did all right," Randy said. "He asked if I thought Bill might be interested in managing the Eagles."

"And what did you say?" Becky asked, a playful gleam in her eye.

"I told him I didn't know," Randy said. "I said he had some of the owners who are for him and others who are unfavorable to the idea. How am I to know?

"Bill can schmooze the stripes off a zebra," Randy said. "I was thinking on the way home about my first visit with him when he came to San Antonio. Can you believe that was twenty years ago? I thought he was the epitome of good manners and gave him the highest marks for the way he treated his elders. There's been a heavy stream of water over the dam since then."

Becky nodded knowingly, reaching across the table carefully with a dinner plate.

"By the way, Bill called you this morning. You may want to give him a return call before we sit down for lunch."

"You know what he wants, don't you?" Randy asked, a hint of resignation in his voice. "At times I think he'd be a good Major League manager, but it's not my decision. Eugene told me last night I shouldn't lobby the owners. 'Speak only if spoken to by the owners' were his exact words. Bill's going to think of me as being unsupportive of his candidacy because I take a noncommittal position."

Randy walked to his private study extending from the master bedroom toward the back of his house. It was his favorite room in the six-thousand-square-foot country-French-styled home, tucked away comfortably in the rolling Texas hills. From his window he could see the redbirds pecking at the seed Becky had poured into the bird feeder earlier that morning. Whitetail deer roamed the hills day and night, adding to the pastoral beauty of his own adaptation of Camelot.

Taking a seat in his large chocolate-brown recliner, Randy touched two buttons on a telephone pad that lay on an end table. A massive audio system turned the entire room into a speaker phone with perfect acoustics.

Two rings.

"Hello?" It was the unmistakable voice of Bill Simons.

Chapter 5

Caught in the Middle

"Do not boast about tomorrow, for you do not know what a day may bring forth."
Proverbs 27:1

Bill Simons was the best baseball player Randy had ever coached. He was any manager's go-to guy. Whenever the Eagles were in a must-win situation, Randy wanted Bill on the mound. The kid was fearless, intimidating, and capable of shutting down the most menacing lineup the opposing team could field on any given day.

From the moment Simons attended his first spring training with the Eagles until he called it a career sixteen seasons later, he was a huge factor in the team's emergence as an annual contender within the National League South. He won three Cy Young awards, recognizing him as being the league's best pitcher; was selected seven times to appear in the annual All-Star game; and had two World Series Championship rings to show for his heroic efforts on Major League Baseball's most venerated stage. He was a pitching phenom.

There was another side to Bill, as Randy had discovered to be true with many of his players. Some were moody, others belligerent, and many had ego problems that were off the charts. Bill's Achilles' heel was his anger. More than once Randy had been called upon to pour olive oil on the wounds Bill had caused with his acerbic tongue. The kid had other issues, to be sure, even some psychosis, but it was his seething wrath that always brought the pot to a boil.

"Hi, Bill. It's Randy, just returning your call. How are things in Austin?"

"All right, I guess," Bill said hesitantly, then cut quickly to the point. "Randy, what's going on with the front office? I feel like I've been left in the dark."

"They aren't telling me much either," Randy said, trying to sound empathetic. He knew what it was like to be left blowing in the wind while others were making major decisions that affected your career.

"I've lobbied your case just about as far as the owners will allow," Randy said. "In no uncertain terms, management has let me know that I will not have much to say about the person who succeeds me. It's not my call." Randy felt like a broken record. He'd said the same words on numerous occasions since he and Bill had first talked about the impending managerial vacancy. He wasn't sure what more he could say, yet he suspected his protégé wanted him to take care of the problem, just as he had tried to do for Bill so many times in years past.

"Where's Gainsworth stand on the issue?" Bill asked. When it came to the Eagles' future, Eugene Gainsworth's presence was characterized as the proverbial elephant in the room. He was a major shareholder in SAE, Incorporated, the holding company that owned the San Antonio Eagle franchise, and no one was allowed to forget that he had funded a huge part of The Nest when it was built more than twenty-five years ago.

More importantly, Eugene Gainsworth was the wealthiest, most prominent citizen in Bexar County. Forty years earlier, when enormous volumes of new oil and gas had been discovered south and west of San Antonio, Gainsworth had moved his independent oil company from Tulsa to South Central Texas. It was a calculated risk, designed by Gainsworth to capitalize on the newly discovered reserves. Over time, the oil tycoon had parlayed a modest fortune into a massive one.

Randy had enjoyed a close relationship with Gainsworth, often hunting and fishing with him in the nearby hills and in Colorado. Theresa Gainsworth, Eugene's glamorous wife, and Becky had become good friends, and the two couples were often seen together at clubs and restaurants throughout San Antonio. Randy was painfully aware that Eugene was not a big fan of Bill Simons.

"I may know more about that next week," Randy said. "We're getting together next Wednesday. Perhaps I'll know something then."

As he hung up the phone, Randy expelled a breath of frustration. The issue of Bill's candidacy posed some serious problems. In his heart, Randy truly believed Bill had earned the right to lead the big league club and was convinced his youth and his drive would be assets for a team that needed a swift kick in the pants. On the other hand, there were a few skeletons in Bill's closet, and they were known to practically everyone who had a vote regarding his future.

* * * * *

Eugene Gainsworth's office was in an executive suite on the top floor of Gainsworth Tower in downtown San Antonio. The spacious reception foyer on the fifty-second floor featured handsome walnut paneling adorned with a brilliant collection of Western and Indian art and opulent European furnishings. The fine collection of sofas, chairs, tables, lamps, and Oriental rugs had been selected by Theresa Gainsworth herself when she and her personal decorator had gone on a scavenger hunt, searching for exquisite pieces throughout England and France. A huge aquarium, filled with colorful fish and other forms of sea life, served as the centerpiece of the room, welcoming all who called upon Texas's wealthiest oil baron.

Randy had been to these offices many times over the past twenty years. Most of his encounters with Gainsworth had been cordial, if not relaxing, but he was wary of those rare occasions when he might catch his friend in an unpleasant frame of mind. No one wanted to be around Eugene Gainsworth when he was in a foul mood.

"Good morning," Gainsworth said as Randy was ushered into the lavishly appointed corner office, which was at least ten times larger than Randy's at the stadium.

"Good morning to you," Randy said, grasping Gainsworth's calloused hand.

"How does it feel to be unemployed?" Gainsworth chuckled. "Is Becky tired of you hanging around the house yet?"

"She's going to give me one more week to find meaningful employment, or I'll have to become her sous-chef and housekeeper, all wrapped up into one." Randy laughed, relieved to see that Gainsworth was in a teasing mood.

Sipping coffee, the friends chatted briefly about their families and a couple of news columns that had appeared on the morning's front page of the *San Antonio Express-News*. After a certain amount of small talk, Gainsworth finally brought the conversation around to the subject that dwarfed all others: finding a suitable successor for Randy's vacated post.

"Have you given any more thought to my advice about Simons?" Gainsworth asked.

"I haven't thought much about anything else," Randy said. "But you and I are going to have to agree to disagree on this one, Eugene. Bill has the skill-set to manage the team. His record in Austin proves he's capable of getting the most out of his players. He has taken a talentless Triple-A team and turned it into a contender. I'm not sure I could have done what he's accomplished in Austin this summer."

"You may be right," Gainsworth said, conceding to Randy's most persuasive argument. "If possessing managerial skills were the only issue, I would feel reasonably good about Bill's chance for success in the Majors. If he were half the manager he was as a player, he would set the league on fire. But until I'm satisfied on some of the other issues regarding his personal habits and behavior over the past few years, I'm reserving judgment.

"There are some other attractive candidates for the job, and I think you need to be more open-minded regarding their suitability for the post."

Local sportswriters had wasted no time filling columns with names of potential field managers who were capable of stepping into the Eagles' current vacancy. Besides Simons' candidacy, there was considerable speculation that Owen Williams, the current manager for the San Diego Padres, might have an interest in making a move. Williams, a native Texan, had coached at the Major League level for seven years and had been named the Padres' manager only two years ago. He brought some proven experience to the table but was not nearly as popular with Eagles fans as Simons.

"Remember what I told you last week, Randy," Gainsworth said. "Don't lobby the issue. Let the owners and front office personnel work the traps on this decision. They're the ones who will ultimately be responsible for the manager's performance on the field. They deserve the right to make the decision without being overly influenced by you."

Randy knew Gainsworth was right to insist that the owners make the decision. He could only wish that his friend's bias against Simons would not preclude the younger man's chance to win the other owners' approval.

Chapter 6

Rookie Romance

"A word fitly spoken is like apples of gold in settings of silver."

Proverbs 25:11

Bill Simons lay restlessly on his king-sized Sealy Posturepedic mattress and replayed the events of the day. Randy had called after visiting with Gainsworth, but the message was not clear as to whether the domineering owner was in Bill's corner or not.

Why does this decision have to be such an ordeal? So mysterious?

There was a time when Bill was confidant of Randy's support, but lately he wasn't so sure. From their telephone visits, it sounded as if Randy was backing Bill's candidacy; then again, he didn't appear to be doing all he could to bring the decision to its rightful conclusion. Something was disturbingly wrong with the entire process. Bill had busted himself for sixteen years as a player with the Eagles and had helped Randy acquire two World Series Championships. The least his former skipper could do was make an all-out effort to see that Bill become heir to the manager's vacated position.

He owes me that!

Bill was forty-three years old and had just completed his fifth season in professional baseball coaching. For the last three years he had been the manager for the Eagles' Triple-A affiliate in Austin, where twice he had led the team to a first-place finish. Although the Falcons had not been successful in post-season play, they had surprised the baseball community by winning the divisional championship. Most of the local sportswriters had predicted the Falcons would finish last, as they had for two consecutive years prior to Bill's arrival in the Texas capital.

If the owners refuse to give me a shot at the San Antonio job, they can take my job with the Falcons and shove it! he thought, his temper increasing. He would leave Austin in a heartbeat.

It was past midnight when Bill closed his eyes, allowing images of his rookie season with the Eagles to dance through his weary mind. He recalled standing agog, admiring his surroundings the moment he stepped between the chalk lines at Gainsworth Stadium. The new facility defined luxurious. Eugene Gainsworth had spared no expense to see that his new ballpark was to baseball what the Dallas Cowboys' "Jerrydome" in Arlington had become to professional football: the ultimate in spectator sport indulgence. The Eagles' massive three-dimensional scoreboard showed instant replays to the naked eye unlike any other scoreboard in the world.

In his first few months with the Eagles, Bill developed the reputation for being a party boy. Following some of the home games, and almost always after a game on the road, he would join a few of his teammates at a bar for lively discussion, a fine cigar, and a few "brewskies." Single, and with no prospects for marriage on the horizon, Bill had no one expecting him at home. Late nights were meant for fun and games; besides, he could sleep in on most mornings.

And then Bill met Sherri Jane Laird, the most beautiful woman in all of God's creation. She had flaming red hair, soft and dimpled cheeks, and blue eyes that sparkled like lights on a Christmas tree.

Where has she been all my life? Bill asked himself upon first laying eyes on her.

Sherri Jane, twenty and on summer break after her junior year at Texas Christian University in Fort Worth, was Wilson Laird's niece. Her famous uncle, working part-time in the Eagles' front office, had made one phone call and secured a summer job for Sherri Jane in the team's public relations office. She had exceptional poise for a woman her age and gained immediate respect from her colleagues for having a strong work ethic. Although she had been popular in sorority life on the TCU campus, she seemed to be shy socially, keeping her guard up around single men, especially members of the baseball community.

Prior to an evening ballgame at Gainsworth Stadium, Sherri Jane had arranged for Bill and Grady McMillon, the Eagles' slick-fielding shortstop, to appear near the third-base dugout to sign autographs for adoring fans. It was all Bill could do to keep his attention on the clamoring fans, who were thrusting their pens and scorecards in his face. All he wanted was a few minutes alone with Sherri Jane. They exchanged only a few words before the moment was over, but their initial meeting was forever etched into his memory.

The next morning, hours before any of the players were scheduled to arrive at the ballpark, Bill called Wilson Laird and asked for a brief appointment. They agreed to meet at Laird's stadium office.

"Come in," Laird hollered from within when Bill knocked. "Door's open."

Bill stepped inside. "Good morning, sir," Bill said. "I'm Bill—"

"I know who you are, young man," Laird said. "Sit down and take a load off. You have a big game tonight." Laird studied Bill briefly. "Not too many rookies with an eight-and-two record at this stage of the season. Congratulations!"

"Thank you, sir," Bill said, flattered that Laird appeared to know more about him than he might have surmised. "I've had lots of support from the team."

"Keep your game face on, son," Laird said. "I think you have a bright future with the Eagles. Now, what can I do for you?"

"Well, sir, uh…" Bill said, stumbling for the right words. "I was wondering if it would be all right if I asked Sherri Jane out for a date. I know management frowns on players dating regular personnel in the club offices, but since Sherri Jane is only a summer intern, I thought there might be an exception made in her case."

"Have you already asked her?" Laird inquired.

"No, sir. I didn't want to get her—or me—in any trouble with you or the club," Bill said as diplomatically as he could muster. "I thought it best to ask you first."

Laird was impressed with the young man. He had courage and good manners all wrapped up into one package. Having been a former Major League manager with a keen eye for talent, Laird knew Bill had the innate ability to become the ace of the Eagles' pitching staff. Sherri Jane's parents would be blown away that the new rookie sensation had shown an interest in their daughter. If Laird didn't acquiesce to the kid's polite request for a date with Sherri Jane, he would be thought of as an old curmudgeon and lose face with his favorite niece.

"I suppose it would be all right for you to ask," Laird said, smirking slightly, "but it's Sherri Jane who'll have to accept your invitation."

"Thank you, sir," Bill said and, without another word, exited the senior statesman's office, too excited to say goodbye.

It took three weeks of coaxing Sherri Jane before she accepted Bill's invitation to go with him on a dinner date. She was spending the summer as a houseguest with her aunt Bonnie and uncle Wil. Until now, no suitors had dared knock at the front door.

Laird greeted Simons as he stood awkwardly on the front porch, shuffling his weight from one foot to the other. Inviting the nervous caller in, Laird had Simons wait a few minutes, allowing Sherri Jane to "put her face on," as he put it. Simons was at the mercy of the older man, and his anxiety increased the longer Sherri Jane primped.

As though she had stepped off the cover of *Vogue*, Sherri Jane emerged, entering the sitting room. Dressed in white designer jeans, a sateen red blouse, and sandals off the rack at Neiman Marcus, Sherri Jane was a knockout.

"Good evening," Bill said, his voice caught in his throat, words stuck in a thoughtless brain. *Way to be smooth,* he thought to himself. "We'll be home by eleven, sir," Bill said abruptly to Sherry Jane's uncle Wil, and the handsome young couple walked out the front door and hopped into Bill's bluebonnet blue-and-silver BMW waiting in Laird's driveway.

That was how it had all begun. Sherri Jane became Bill's inspiration for the remainder of the season. He pitched every game with the added incentive of impressing the young woman who had unexpectedly walked into his life. He took special delight when Randy Dobson or one of his teammates made mention of his dating Laird's niece.

Bill finished the season with a record of 19-4 and an ERA of 2.89. He was runner-up in the voting for Rookie of the Year, losing to Pittsburgh's amazing young shortstop, Manny Diaz, who hit .345, stole forty-two bases, and won the coveted Gold Glove Award. Although Bill had not won the trophy, he had great satisfaction in the outcome of his first season in Major League Baseball.

It had been a wonderful summer on the baseball field, and after meeting Sherri Jane, it had been an even better summer off the field.

Who needs that Rookie of the Year trophy? he mused to himself. *I'm dating a bombshell. How can it get any better than this?*

Chapter 7

Taking the Plunge

"He who finds a wife finds a good thing and obtains favor from the Lord."
                                    Proverbs 18:22

Sherri Jane returned to Fort Worth in late August to begin her senior year at TCU. With one month of the baseball season remaining, Bill had no choice except to let her go, promising to call, e-mail, and text often. The thought of Sherri Jane walking across campus and turning the heads of all the fraternity boys sent shivers down his spine. If he had so much as heard a whisper of her dating one of those admirers, he would have plummeted into a rage. Sherri Jane was his girl!

On the last weekend in September, when Bill was scheduled to pitch against the Houston Astros, Sherri Jane and two of her sorority sisters made a weekend trip to San Antonio. The game turned into a nightmare. Bill experienced his roughest outing of the season, giving up seven earned runs in three innings. When he walked the first two hitters he faced in the top of the fourth inning, Randy pulled him from the game.

"That's it tonight, kid," Randy said, taking the ball from Bill and motioning toward the dugout. The Eagles' manager had never seen his rookie sensation so flustered in a ballgame, but he knew even the best pitchers had a few off nights.

Bill was embarrassed by his performance, and even more so by Randy pulling him from the game so early in the contest. He stormed off the mound, looking steadily at the ground while pounding his fist into his glove.

What is Randy trying to do to me? He's making me look like a fool in front of Sherri Jane and her friends.

As Bill entered the dugout, he threw his glove under the bench, shouted an uncharacteristic expletive, and muttered some hateful thoughts about Randy under his breath. The meltdown was witnessed by his teammates and many of the spectators in the stands.

Bill ignored Sherri Jane's calls that weekend and chose not see her.

Although the Eagles finished the season with their best record in franchise history, they were nudged out of the playoffs by the Houston Astros, who won twelve of their last fourteen games to claim the National League's Southern Division championship. The Eagle players and coaches cleaned out their lockers, promising each other to keep up their physical conditioning program during the winter and to report to spring training next year with fresh resolve to win the National League pennant.

Bill wasted no time in making a trip to Fort Worth. He and Sherri Jane still e-mailed one another and texted some, but they had cut back on phone calls since the day of Bill's tantrum in the dugout. Now the young suitor was anxious to see if the couple had a future together, and there was no way to settle the issue long distance.

"Sherri Jane. It's me," Bill said over his cell phone. "I just crossed the Tarrant County line and thought we could have some time together the next few days."

His chipper greeting was met with silence, the pause pregnant with uncertainty.

"I want to," Sherri Jane said, her voice soft and warm enough to melt butter, "but I'm in the middle of six-week exams, Bill, and I couldn't possibly see you the next two days. If you'd called me earlier, I could have spared you the trip."

Bill couldn't believe it. He had driven all the way to Fort Worth to see Sherri Jane, and she was choosing exams over spending time with him. He may as well have been blasted by a policeman's Taser gun.

Alone in his car, Bill slammed his cell phone on the floor, shouting every vile word he knew. He tore out of a shopping center parking lot in his BMW, pressed the accelerator to the floorboard, and did not stop until a Texas Ranger pulled him over five miles south of Burleson.

A month passed before Bill mustered the courage to call Sherri Jane. They had not spoken to one another since that revolting night. As he dialed the familiar number, he reached deep inside for courage to make amends for his behavior.

"Sherri Jane?"

"Hi, Bill," she answered guardedly.

"Listen, Sherri Jane, I'm embarrassed for the way I've acted the past few weeks. I've been a real jerk. Can you forgive me?"

"Bill, I've missed you this fall. If I had it to do over, I would have forgotten about the silly exams and made time to see you when you came to Fort Worth. You need to forgive me too, okay?"

Having patched up their differences, Bill and Sherri Jane renewed their dating pattern, going to a few of her sorority events and attending the last TCU Horned Frog football game of the season. Bill was a big hit with the collegians, male and female alike. He enjoyed being the center of attention with Sherri Jane's friends, but he was pleased even more that his relationship with his blue-eyed angel was moving in the right direction.

One evening, a week before Christmas, Bill took Sherri Jane to dinner at the Colonial Country Club in Fort Worth. This hallowed shrine, former home of the PGA's legendary golfer the late Ben Hogan, was accessible to Bill through some well-heeled Eagle fans who happened to be members of the club. He had traded some autographed bats, balls, and jerseys for the privilege of using their membership to dine at the club.

A tall, middle-aged Italian headwaiter, dressed in black-tie and tuxedo, welcomed the handsome couple into the main dining room. "Good evening. Two for dinner?"

"Yes, and could I ask you a favor?" Bill extended his hand, a crisp one hundred-dollar bill tucked inside the palm. "We need to be off to the side—at a corner table, away from the traffic." Bill could only imagine the circus that would ensue if the autograph seekers discovered him in the dining room.

The *Maître d'* studied the room and then turned toward Bill and said, "Please, follow me." He led Bill and Sherri Jane to an alcove. A small table covered with a smartly pressed white linen cloth was adorned with snowy-white china rimmed in a broad navy blue stripe, polished sterling silver tableware atop white linen napkins, an array of sparkling crystal glasses and goblets, and a small centerpiece of red roses peeking out of a dainty arrangement of white baby's breath and green lemon leaves.

"Excellent," Bill said, nodding to the *Maître d'* as he pulled out a chair for Sherri Jane. "This is just what I had in mind."

The couple took a few moments to admire the room and consider its storied past.

"It's so elegant," Sherri Jane said. "What a lovely place you have chosen for dinner."

"I thought you'd like it." Charmingly, he asked, "Do you mind if I order for you tonight, Sherri Jane?"

"I'd love for you to," she whispered.

Bill briefly scanned the menu and then summoned the waiter to the table. He ordered shrimp cocktail, Caesar salad, prime rib to be broiled medium rare, loaded baked potatoes, and asparagus spears. The waiter, sans pad and pencil, nodded as he took mental note of each item. Moving professionally around the table, he filled the water glasses, suggested a California red wine to accompany the meal, and then left the couple alone for a few minutes as he returned to the kitchen with their order.

Left alone with his beautiful belle, Bill was captivated by Sherri Jane's dancing blue eyes and the blush of her creamy smooth cheeks. Her smile cast a glow about the table, adding another dimension to the enchanting ambience that already existed in the dining room. Listening to her, he caught every third word as she shared a story of one of her sorority sisters who had left during the past week on a cruise in the Caribbean. The reverie broke only when the waiter returned with the shrimp cocktails and began to pour each of them a glass of wine.

After finishing their salads, Bill and Sherri Jane admired the entrees as the head waiter presented the elegantly decorated plates before them. The beef was cooked to perfection, and the potatoes were offered with every possible topping, including Bill's favorite, bits of French-fried onion rings.

"Shall we?" Bill said, cutting into his prime rib. After a single bite, Sherri Jane began to choke, unable to get her breath.

"Sherri Jane, are you okay?!" Panicked, Bill readied to administer the Heimlich maneuver.

Sherri Jane shook her head, pointing to her plate. She had taken a generous bite of horseradish, the potent condiment, clearly mistaking it for something else, and it had cleared out every sinus cavity in her head. Her blue eyes filled with tears as she quickly quenched the burn with a whole glass of ice water. Five minutes passed before she could utter a single word.

"Are you going to be all right?" Bill asked, trying not to laugh.

Sherri Jane nodded, embarrassed at her own faux pas, and whispered, "No more horseradish."

The crisis passed, and the two starlets finished their meal, enjoying each bite and commending the chef to their waiter. A small combo began to play light dinner music in the background.

Bill, using his napkin to wipe the last bit of *au jus* from his mouth, called for dessert. He had chosen one of his all-time favorites: Cherries Jubilee. When the waiter returned, placing the red and white concoction in front of the two diners, Sherri Jane's eyes grew as wide as silver dollars. Her plate had a small, but impressive gift box next to the Jubilee.

"Well, are you going to open it?" Bill asked.

Tears filled Sherri Jane's eyes, her surprise evident in the thrill of the moment. She had not expected a gift, much less a box marked with the distinctive initials signifying a present that had been purchased from Tiffany's. With shaking hands she lifted the lid of the jewelry box to discover the most astonishing diamond ring she had ever seen.

"Sherri Jane, will you marry me?"

Chapter 8

A Bad Day at Wrigley

"A wise son heeds his father's instruction,
but a scoffer does not listen to rebuke."
Proverbs 13:1

Sherri Jane accepted Bill's proposal for marriage, making both of them among the happiest people on the planet. They preferred to set an early wedding date, but circumstances dictated otherwise. Bill was scheduled to report for spring training in seven weeks, and once the baseball season began, there would be no way to squeeze in a wedding. Sherri Jane was pre-enrolled for her last semester at TCU, planning to graduate in early May. Assessing their options, they chose a December wedding date, one year to the day from the memorable evening they had celebrated at the Colonial Country Club.

* * * * *

From the moment players began to arrive at spring training camp, a new attitude permeated the Eagles' locker room. Thanks in large measure to its rookie pitching sensation, Bill Simons, the team knew it had made enormous strides toward qualifying for the playoffs the previous summer. More would be expected of the young star this year, and Bill was eager to deliver on his teammates' expectations.

Roy S. Westbrooke was back for his sixteenth consecutive year as the Eagles' pitching coach. Admired throughout the league for his incomparable ability to develop young players, Westbrooke tackled each season with boundless enthusiasm. This year he wanted to help Bill add a new pitch to his formidable arsenal of hurling weapons.

"Do you remember watching Mariano Rivera when you were a kid?" Westbrooke asked Bill as they met on the training mound.

"Sure," Bill said. "I've always been a Yankees fan. He had that incredible cutter."

Rivera, inducted into the National Baseball Hall of Fame after his playing days were over, had perfected a cut-fastball that became his signature pitch. All batters who faced him knew the pitch was coming, but most of them could not make enough contact with the ball to do any damage. Rivera ended his career as the all-time "saves" champion, having completed more games than any other pitcher in Major League history.

"Well, that's what we want to work on this year," Westbrooke said, gripping the baseball. "You already have an excellent fastball with good movement on it, a decent curveball that'll get better this year, and your changeup is as good as any in the league. If you can develop a Major League cutter to go with your other pitches, you'll give the hitters some serious aggravation this summer."

Bill accepted his coach's challenge and began throwing a hard cutter that had great promise. It had just enough movement to keep right-handed hitters off stride. With four strong pitches under his command, Bill was ready for the regular season to begin.

Opening Day at Gainsworth Stadium was the biggest celebration San Antonio had experienced since the Spurs had won their last NBA championship. The Eagles' front office, sparing no expense, had been planning the event for months. The colossal three-dimensional scoreboard was programmed to work overtime, showing clips from the team's past seasons and a brief salute from the Honorable John

F. Ohlmstead, President of the United States. Wilson Laird and Randy Dobson, the only men to serve as Eagles' managers, rode onto the field in bluebonnet blue-and-silver Mercedes convertibles, welcomed by a thunderous ovation.

Randy and Eugene Gainsworth had spent weeks during the winter selling season tickets to the major corporate enterprises in South Central Texas. The two men made an irresistible sales force, and the fruit of those efforts now sat in the stands. A record crowd of 53,344 witnessed the Opening Day spectacle and were rewarded with a 7-to-1 Eagles' victory over the Atlanta Braves.

Randy named Bill as his starting pitcher in the second game against the Braves. Sherri Jane made the trip from Fort Worth to root for Bill in his first start of the season. She, along with her uncle Wil and aunt Bonnie, sat with Eugene and Theresa Gainsworth in the owner's plush executive suite.

"How many more weeks until graduation?" Wilson Laird asked.

"Six weeks, Uncle Wil," Sherri Jane said, beaming. "Are you and Aunt Bonnie coming for commencement exercises?"

"I told your dad we would meet them there," Laird said.

"What I want to know about is the wedding," Bonnie said. "Did I hear something about a December date?"

"December 18th. Can you believe it?" Sherri Jane asked, her voice laced with genuine excitement. "Bill thinks we should elope, but I told him I wanted a church wedding with all the bells and whistles."

As Sherrie Jane described further details of the upcoming ceremony to her aunt Bonnie, she was interrupted by the announcement from the stadium announcer, asking that all spectators rise for the singing of the National Anthem. As the song came to an end, the umpire's guttural call, "Play ball!" prompted cheering from the crowd. Game two in the three-game series was under way!

Bill breezed through the first five innings without allowing a base runner. In the top half of the sixth, the Braves' leadoff hitter managed a bloop single to centerfield, but he was erased on a ground ball double-play, short-to-second-to-first. The Eagles scored two runs in their half of the third inning and another in the seventh. That was all Bill needed as he tossed a one-hit shutout for the Eagles' second win of the young season.

At the end of April, the Eagles were perched in first place in the National League South with a record of twenty wins and five losses. Bill won four of his five starting assignments in April, the fifth resulting in no decision for him, but a victory for the team when utility-man Red Mosier came off the bench, driving in the winning run with a pinch-hit single to right field in the bottom of the twelfth inning. Bill was pitching well, and he knew it; his self-confidence was rising every day.

Sherri Jane graduated from TCU with honors in May, but Bill had been unable to attend the commencement program because the Eagles were on a road trip to the West Coast. She had spent a few weeks looking for a job but decided not to press the issue too hard because she had plenty to do in anticipation of the wedding.

Besides, she thought, *Bill makes more than enough for both of us.*

On the second day of June, Bill was on the mound at Wrigley Field, pitching against the Chicago Cubs, who were holding on to first place in the National League North. He did not appear to have good command of his pitches that warm afternoon. Through five innings, Bill had allowed seven base hits, three walks, and four earned runs. The Eagles and Cubs were tied as Bill threw his first pitch in the bottom half of the sixth inning. He walked the lead-off man and hit the next hitter on the wrist with a curveball that didn't break.

"Time!" Randy called, striding to the mound. "Heat getting to you, Bill?"

"I'm fine," Bill said, not wanting to be lifted without the opportunity for a win.

"Let's call it a day," Randy said, reaching for the baseball.

Bill held on to the little white sphere for a few seconds too long, embarrassing Randy and causing his teammates some angst. Finally, he flipped the ball in Randy's general direction and stalked off the mound.

The Cub fans were giving the young hurler an earful as he approached the dugout. Bill took a brief look into the crowd, unable to ignore their heckling. He focused on no one in particular and failed to notice an elderly gentleman slumped in his seat in the fifth row, wearing an Eagles cap, wiping tears from his eyes.

Upon reaching the dugout, Bill grabbed a towel and swiped at the sweat on his face, then took a seat at the end of the bench, far removed from any of the other players. He wanted no consolation from anyone. He was sure he could have shut down the rally if Randy had trusted him with the baseball. When the next hitter knocked the relief pitcher's first offering well beyond Wrigley Field's fabled ivy-covered centerfield wall, Bill stormed through the dugout, cursing everything in sight: coaches, relief pitchers, umpires, even the batboy, who happened to be in Bill's way as he exited toward the clubhouse.

The next day, Randy asked Bill to come by his office for a visit.

"I know you didn't want to leave the game," Randy said, "but as manager, I can't have you or anyone else on this team pull a stunt like you did yesterday. When I ask for the baseball, I expect it to be placed in my hand immediately. And as far as these temper tantrums are concerned, they better stop or you'll lose all credibility with me and with your teammates. I'm as impressed as the next fellow with your talent, Bill, but you've got to learn to deal with your anger or it'll destroy you. You're a professional! You hear me?"

Bill refused to look at Randy, his eyes fixed on the floor in front of him.

"I hear you," he muttered. "But what made you think George Mendel had a better chance of getting Cervantes out than I did?" Unable to contain his emotions, Bill's voice rose as angry words spewed from his mouth. "He threw him a gopher ball, Randy, smack dab down the middle of the plate. A high school pitcher could've thrown that pitch."

"You're not listening to me," Randy said, as calmly as possible. "I regret it, Bill, but I'm fining you ten thousand dollars and expect you to apologize to your teammates before tomorrow's game."

Bill groaned, contemptuous.

"Do you understand?"

"Whatever," he said. "Is that all?"

"That's all," Randy said, hopeful he'd not done more harm than good.

Chapter 9

A Secret Exposed

"Whoever guards his mouth and tongue keeps his soul from troubles."
Proverbs 21:23

Bill spent the next few days sulking, unable to accept Randy's reprimand and the ten thousand-dollar fine. For him, it wasn't about the money; he could pay the fine as easily as most people paid parking tickets, but it was the principle of the matter. In his eyes, he had done nothing wrong. Randy had overreacted, and Bill was the victim of his manager's overreaching autocratic behavior.

Roy Westbrooke, concerned about the sullen mood of one of his starting pitchers, decided it was time to have a visit with Randy. He knocked on the manager's office door, opening it as he walked in.

"Got a minute?" he asked, sitting down in an armchair before Randy could reply.

"What's on your mind?" Randy asked, scribbling notes on a yellow legal pad.

"It's Bill," Roy said. "We need to work through this issue concerning Bill. The kid's become a recluse, hardly says a word to anyone. Some of the players are beginning to feel sorry for him and think you may have overreacted."

"Is that how you see it?" Randy asked, knowing Roy was a strong authoritarian himself but also a man who tried to keep peace in the clubhouse.

"No, not really," Roy said. "He deserved the warning, and I suppose the fine was in order too. But there's something about Bill's past you may not know."

"Like what?"

"According to Wil Laird, Bill's dad left him and his mother when the kid was nine years old, ran off with some woman and moved to California. Never came back to see Bill while he was growing up. Bill hates his dad and wishes he were dead. Heck, maybe he is dead, who knows? I have the feeling he may be transferring some of his emotional vitriol to guys like you and me when we have cause to discipline him."

Roy's words settled heavily on Randy's heart. He hadn't taken the time to delve into Bill's past, remembering only now that the kid had mentioned taking his *mom* to see the Alamo a few years ago but had never uttered a word about his *dad*.

That should've been my first clue.

Randy had an immediate pang of remorse, disappointed he had not discovered this piece of information earlier. He never wanted to smother his players by prying into their personal lives, but neither did he want to become one of those heartless managers, caring less what demons might be haunting the men on his roster.

"You may be on to something, Roy," Randy said. "Thanks for filling me in. I'll see what I can do."

The next morning, Randy called Bill to his office. He wasn't sure how to begin the conversation, but the sooner the matter was settled, the better for Randy, Bill, and the entire team.

"Bill, I have decided to cancel the fine," Randy said. "I probably overreacted and want to get it behind us before it gets out of hand."

Bill sat in his chair stoically.

"Let's write it off as an anomaly in our working relationship," Randy said, "rather than it becoming our normal way of dealing with one another. Fair enough?"

"Sure, skipper."

"Bill," Randy said, hesitating, "I just learned yesterday about your dad." Bill flinched, going rigid in his chair.

"What does he have to do with anything?"

"Nothing, really," Randy said tentatively. "I just want to let you know that I care about you as a person, not just as a ball player. I'm here for you if you need me for anything...*anything*."

"How'd you find out about my dad?" Bill asked demandingly.

Randy paused for a moment, debating whether it was appropriate to acknowledge his sources. He decided it was best not to play "I've got a secret." Roy knew he had put Randy in a delicate position and was strong enough to take the hit if Bill came after him.

"Roy keeps his ear to the ground better than I do," Randy confessed. "He may have picked up something from Wil Laird."

Sherri Jane! Bill's eyes flashed wildly. *She's the only one I've ever talked to about my dad, and she told her uncle Wil. She's going to hear about this, about airing out the details of my personal life. What else has she told?!*

"You're scheduled to start Friday against the Reds," Randy said, breaking Bill's mental monologue. "Are you good with that, or do you need another day to flush this whole issue through the system?"

"I'll be ready to pitch whenever you give me the rock and tell me it's my turn to throw," Bill said, like a seasoned veteran.

Bill stood and shook Randy's outstretched hand. The boil had been lanced, and Randy was hopeful it would be able to heal.

* * * * *

As the season wore on, the Eagles held a slight lead in their division. Once again, the Astros made a late run for the flag, but strong pitching and timely hitting from the middle of the Eagles' lineup kept Randy's club three games ahead of the pack. Bill was carrying his share of the load, winning his twentieth game on September 3rd and scheduled to start five more times before the regular season finale.

When San Antonio lost three consecutive games to the Cardinals in St. Louis, the divisional race was tied, the Eagles and Houston sharing the lead. The two teams were scheduled to play a three-game series at Gainsworth Stadium for the title.

Game one belonged to the Eagles in a romp. Horace Clevenger, San Antonio's muscular first-baseman, launched a towering shot over the right-field scoreboard with bases loaded in the first inning. The Eagles scored in each of the next five innings, winning by a lopsided score of thirteen to three. The club needed to win one of its next two games to claim the division.

Game two was a much closer contest. Tied six to six going into the top of the ninth inning, the Eagles committed two errors, resulting in two unearned runs, and they lost the nail-biter eight to six. The whole season had come down to Sunday's finale, with Bill Simons facing the Astros' flame-throwing lefty, Keith Karnes.

Regardless of the game's outcome, Bill had claimed his place among the Major League's pitching elite. In July, he had been selected to pitch in the annual All-Star classic at Yankee Stadium. The National League had prevailed four to three, and Bill had recorded two strikeouts to preserve the victory in the bottom of the ninth inning. He brought a record of twenty-three wins and seven losses into the regular season finale, having lowered his earned-run average to 2.27. The kid from Kansas was becoming immensely popular with San Antonio fans.

Sherri Jane had found an apartment in San Antonio and made it a priority to be at every home game Bill pitched. She'd been busy making plans for the wedding but tried not to bother Bill with too many of the details. He needed to keep his focus on baseball for the next few weeks. If the Eagles could get past Houston, they would be in the National League play-offs for the first time in franchise history. Sunday's game would decide their fate.

As the final game entered the ninth inning, tension in the stands was palpable. Two singles, a sacrifice bunt, and a sacrifice fly gave the Eagles a 1-0 lead in the sixth. Bill shut down the Astros' bats, allowing three scattered singles over eight innings, but Houston had not been able to advance any runner past first base.

The Astros had the top of their batting order coming to the plate in the last frame. The leadoff hitter, Manny Lopez, was leading the league with seventy-eight steals in eighty-two attempts. On the first pitch, Lopez laid down a perfect bunt, near the third base foul line. Winston Lee, the Eagles' third-baseman, made a one-handed pickup of the ball, throwing in the same motion, but Lopez beat the throw by a step. A man on first and nobody out.

Bill made two throws to first base, keeping Lopez from getting too large of a lead, but it was to no avail. The speedster took off for second base on Bill's first pitch to the plate, and, diving headfirst into the bag, he was safe with room to spare. A man on second and nobody out.

From the corner of his eye, Bill saw Randy emerge from the dugout, striding rather deliberately to the mound. Under his breath, he let out a groan. He desperately wanted to finish the game.

"You got anything left, or should we call it a day?" Randy asked.

"I'd like to finish what I started," Bill said confidently.

"It's all yours, Bill." Randy grinned. "Let's wrap this one up and see what those playoffs are all about."

Bill drew upon every ounce of strength he possessed to strike out the next three batters on ten pitches. The last strike was the best cutter he had thrown all year.

Even Mariano Rivera would have been proud of that pitch, he thought to himself, swaggering triumphantly into the dugout.

The San Antonio Eagles, champions of the National League South, were post-season-playoffs bound.

CHAPTER 10

A Stranger at the Door

> "There is a generation that curses its father and does not bless its mother."
>
> Proverbs 30:11

Bill found it hard to get much sleep Sunday night following the title-clenching win over the Astros. He replayed the game over and over in his mind. When he awoke Monday morning a few minutes past five, every muscle in his body ached, and sweat had soaked his T-shirt and pajama bottoms.

After taking a warm shower and getting dressed for the day, Bill brewed a pot of Colombian Roast Starbucks Coffee and picked up the newspaper lying on his front porch. A photo on page one instantly brought a smile to his face; he was the toast of the town.

The early edition of the *San Antonio Express-News* carried two front-page stories about the Eagles' victory over the Astros and a color photo of Bill Simons in full stride, delivering his opening pitch toward home plate. For those who did not know Simons prior to Sunday's game, they were beginning to get the picture. The kid had become the team's ace, notching twenty-four victories and 215 strikeouts during the regular season; and with yesterday's victory, he had led the Eagles into their first post-season competition.

After the game, Bill had been overwhelmed with interviews by sportswriters from all over the country. They asked specific questions about the game he had just won, probed gently into his personal life, and solicited his opinion about the upcoming playoff series with the St. Louis Cardinals. He relished the moment, enjoying the limelight, the adulation, and the circus-like atmosphere that surrounded him. To everyone holding a notepad or a microphone he repeated his true feelings: *This is what baseball is all about.*

The Cardinals had caught the Chicago Cubs on the last week of the season, once again dashing the hope of the hapless Cubs being able to play in a World Series. For more than a century, Chicago had been the doormat of the National League. The last time the

Cubs had won a World Series was 1908, resulting in the longest streak of failure and frustration in Major League Baseball history.

St. Louis, on the other hand, had enjoyed a surprisingly good year. The Cardinals had not been predicted to finish higher than third in the National League North, and they had not qualified for the playoffs since 2016. Nonetheless, eleven World Series Championship banners flew on the flagpoles in Busch Stadium. If nothing more than tradition, the Redbirds would be formidable post-season foes for the inexperienced Eagles.

Having won two more regular season games than the Eagles, St. Louis had the home-field advantage and would host the first two games of a seven-game series in Busch Stadium. Bill would not be on the mound in either of those games because his arm would require four days' rest following his victory over the Astros. Randy had designated Bill as the starting pitcher in game three, the first playoff game ever played at Gainsworth Stadium.

The Eagles booked a charter flight to St. Louis for 3:00 p.m. on Monday. Randy wanted the team to have a full day on Tuesday for workouts, including infield-outfield drills and batting practice. Game one was a late-afternoon start on Wednesday.

Sherri Jane, who had celebrated with Bill and the team until almost midnight the night before, had promised to pick him up at his house around 9:00 on Monday morning and chauffeur him to Gainsworth Stadium. Randy had called a team meeting for eleven sharp, and Bill wanted to arrive at the clubhouse early enough to receive his share of the day's kudos and high-fives. At ten minutes until nine, Bill's doorbell rang.

Sherri Jane, right on time, he thought.

When Bill opened the door, he was surprised to see someone other than Sherri Jane standing on his doorstep: an overweight elderly man wearing an Eagles' baseball cap and a bluebonnet blue Eagles' sweatshirt. From all appearances, he was just another fan going to unbelievable lengths to get an autograph.

"Good morning, Bill," the bearded stranger said with a warm smile. There was something eerily familiar about his face.

"Good morning," Bill said, annoyed by the unexpected interruption.

"You don't recognize me, do you, Bill?" the man asked.

Bill racked his brain, searching for an answer to who the familiar stranger might be. Maybe they had met at a Fan-Fare event or at one of the local Eagle promotional cavalcades. His features reminded him of someone he knew, but he couldn't say he actually recognized him.

"No, I guess not," Bill said, a poor attempt at masking his irritation.

"I'm...your father."

The intense pain of his father's desertion fifteen years ago coursed through Bill's emotional psyche like a bullet fired from a revolver at close range. The man standing on his doorstep had been both the target and the cause of Bill's wrath since he was a kid. Now this fiend, this womanizing child abandoner, had the nerve to stand in front of him, trying to look cheery. Did he have no shame?

Bill was stunned, at a loss for words, heat snaking up the nape of his neck like smoke pouring through a chimney.

How dare this...this demon who has haunted me for so many years suddenly appear at my front door!

"I have nothing to say to you!" Bill yelled, baring his teeth. He had often wondered what he would say to his father if and when he ever encountered him. Now here he was, apparently trying to bask in the limelight of Bill's success. He appeared to Bill as nothing more than one of the derelicts who made their homes on the streets and under the bridges in

San Antonio. He could have been at any street corner begging for handouts, wearing a sign that said, "Feed me. My son is Bill Simons."

"But Bill—"

"Get off my property!" Bill screamed. "I don't ever want to see you here again!" It was all Bill could do not to punch the disheveled intruder in his cheesy-looking face. "I hate you! Do you understand? I hate you!"

His father winced at the outburst, looked at Bill for a moment, and then turned and walked away to the dilapidated gray Dodge coupe that was parked in Bill's driveway. The old man opened the door, looked back over his shoulder at Bill one more time, and slid into the car. He turned the key, the car's engine growling, frame rattling. A wisp of black smoke escaped from the exhaust pipe and the car backfired, startling a pair of robins that had been grubbing in Bill's front yard.

"If you come here again, I'll call the police!" Bill yelled as his father backed the car out of the driveway and onto the street.

"What was that all about?" Sherri Jane asked, running up the sidewalk. "Did he threaten you? Bill, did he hurt you? Who is he?"

Bill held open the front door, allowing Sherri Jane to enter the house before he followed, closing the door and locking it behind him. A tremor coursed through his entire body, leaving his limbs tingling and weak.

"He said he was my father," Bill said quietly, his emotion drained by the unexpected reunion with a man he abhorred. "As far as I'm concerned, I have no father."

Sherri Jane reached for Bill, wanting to hug him tightly around his neck, but Bill jerked his head, pulling away from her.

"I'm sorry, Bill. I'm so sorry you had to meet him like this. Can we talk about it?"

For years, Bill had borne the matter of his father privately and preferred to keep it that way. He had no use for the shrinks who tried to get clients to work through difficult relationships. His father was a scoundrel for leaving his family, and time had not changed the way Bill felt about him. He knew Sherri Jane was trying to be empathetic, but he wanted her to butt out.

"I'd rather not, Sherri Jane," Bill said emphatically. "This is my issue, and I am not in a mood to discuss it. Furthermore, I don't want you sharing matters like this with your uncle Wil. Just leave it alone."

Sherri Jane was stung by Bill's rebuke. She wanted to console him, but he had hurt her feelings. She dropped her head, wiped away a tear with the back of her hand, and looked toward the front door, her keys in hand.

"Ready to go to the stadium?"

*   *   *   *   *

The playoff series with St. Louis did not go well for the Eagles. The young team had played with enormous heart to get into the post-season but did not appear to have enough fuel in the tank to advance past the first round. The Cardinals overpowered the visitors in Busch Stadium, smashing three homeruns in each of the first two games, winning both seven to two.

When the series moved to Texas, the Eagles had their backs against the wall. They would need to win four of the next five games and were hoping for a sweep in Gainsworth Stadium. Bill performed admirably in the third game—a pitching duel that the Eagles won two to one—but he did not factor in the decision. Randy had lifted him in favor of a pinch-hitter in the eighth inning, and the Eagles won the game on Horace Clevenger's solo homerun in the bottom of the ninth.

From that moment on, the series belonged to St. Louis. The Cardinals won games four and five, both shutouts, and advanced to the National League Championship Series against the New York Mets.

The Eagles' grueling season had come to an abrupt end. It was a bittersweet conclusion for Randy and his team. They had accomplished more than any Eagle squad had achieved in the past, yet they had missed their finest opportunity to play for a National League pennant and perhaps a World Series Championship. Those honors would have to wait for another year.

At the season's end, Bill and Sherri Jane had two months to prepare for their wedding.

"Now we can finally think about something besides baseball," Sherri Jane said teasingly as she presented Bill with his list of prenuptial assignments, all to be completed prior to the hallowed event.

Chapter 11

An Unforgettable Ceremony

> "Pride goes before destruction and a haughty spirit before a fall."
>
> **Proverbs 16:18**

"They're beautiful!" Sherri Jane said as she opened another wedding present. "And exactly the colors Bill and I have chosen for our master bathroom. Thank you, Cindy. I love the monograms."

Becky Dobson had offered to host a bridal shower for Sherri Jane, and many of the women who attended were spouses of the Eagles' players or of personnel who worked in the front office. Bonnie Laird was helping her niece keep track of the presents and the names of those who were listed on the gift cards.

When the final package was opened, Becky suggested the ladies share stories of surprises they had experienced within the first three months of their marriages.

"I was shocked that Horace had no handyman skills," Megan Clevenger said. "He could hardly screw in a light bulb."

"When we first married, your uncle Wil was a better cook than I was," Aunt Bonnie said. "He loved to grill steaks and chicken on the patio, and he knew his way around the kitchen too."

Other women joined in the fun, telling humorous stories about their husbands, either deficiencies or exceptional talents, as the case may be.

Sharon McMillon, whose husband, Grady, had led the Eagles in hitting the past year, said her surprise was in learning how dysfunctional Grady's family had turned out to be.

"His mother still has her apron strings around Grady, and his dad constantly meddles in our marriage," Sharon said. "I thought we were supposed to be independent from our parents once we got married."

"I don't think we will have to worry about Bill's parents," Sherri Jane said smugly. "He hates his dad and hardly ever mentions his mother. Independence won't be a problem for us."

Sherri Jane's revelation about Bill and his dad cast a pall over the room, causing her to feel uncomfortably self-conscious. She needed to retract her comment but knew that would only make matters worse.

"Let's all come into the dining room and have some cake," Becky, ever the hostess, said, rescuing Sherri Jane as she stood and walked into the next room.

* * * * *

Sherri Jane had chosen to have her wedding in Fort Worth so that many of her sorority sisters and other friends from TCU could be in attendance. Her parents, who once lived in Dallas, had many acquaintances in the Metroplex. They arrived from California two weeks early to attend a few pre-wedding events and visit old friends.

December weather in Texas can be all over the map, from balmy sunshine to freezing rain and drizzle. Fortunately for Sherri Jane and Bill, the wedding day forecast called for sunshine, calm winds, and a high of 69 degrees. All systems were go.

Sherri Jane had selected South University Church of Christ, five blocks from TCU's campus, as the venue for the celebratory event. The university life minister, Robin Gage, had befriended Sherri Jane while she was a student. Seven months ago, she and Bill had asked him to officiate at their wedding ceremony, and he gladly agreed to do so. Robin, who grew up in Austin, was an avid San Antonio Eagles fan and stood in awe of Bill whenever in his presence.

A small *a cappella* choral ensemble of university students sang contemporary love ballads and Broadway show music as the final guests were ushered into the church's spacious auditorium. Flowers and candles, featuring the Eagles' bluebonnet blue and silver, were tastefully arranged across the wide stage. Once Bill's mother and Sherri Jane's grandparents and parents were seated, the ceremony began.

Bill stood next to the minister, peering down the center aisle, as one bridesmaid after another took her place opposite the groom and his groomsmen. Whatever Bonnie Laird may have lacked in her culinary skills, she had more than made up for with the sewing machine. As a special gift to her niece, Bonnie had personally sewn all five of the bridesmaids' dresses and made a sixth for the flower girl. In keeping with Sherri Jane's wishes, the dresses were also bluebonnet blue, trimmed with a silver sash around the waist and a silver bow on the back.

The minister asked the audience to stand, and Sherri Jane, escorted by her father, began the long walk down the center aisle. Bill flashed a million-dollar smile the moment he first saw his bride. Her red hair, styled in long ringlets, much like a movie star's coiffure, offset against the pure white dress made for an unbelievable sight. He bit hard on his lower lip to keep tears from welling up in his eyes. Now here she was, the woman he knew to be the love of his life, standing next to him and her father at the altar.

Being wintertime, there was no air-conditioning in the auditorium, and Bill was beginning to feel the heat. He and his groomsmen had been standing at rigid attention like a troop of enlisted recruits in boot camp, and his muscles were beginning to cramp. He needed a glass of cold water, but there was no way to slake his thirst. The main act was underway, and he was a principal character in a starring role.

Bill found it difficult to concentrate on all that Robin Gage was saying. He faintly heard Robin mention "leaving father and mother...."

Well, of course, he thought. *I did that years ago.* As Robin began to cite a passage from the Bible, Bill swayed gently.

The next thing Bill recalled, he was lying on the floor, a man he did not know applying an ice-cold towel to his forehead. He raised his hand to touch his head, which hurt like someone had hit him with a baseball bat.

"Bill, are you all right?" He recognized Randy Dobson's familiar voice. "How many fingers am I holding up?" Bill knew it was either two or three, but what difference did it really make?

As Robin had led the couple through their vows, Bill had allowed his knees to lock, cutting off normal blood circulation to his body. When blood rushed from his head, Bill fainted, falling like a piece of timber cleared by a woodcutter's chainsaw. Only a carpeted floor had saved Bill from serious injury.

"I've heard of a groom having cold feet." Grady McMillon chortled as he saw that Bill was going to be okay. "But you take the prize for trying to bail out at the last minute. Sherri Jane might have some second thoughts about her knight in shining armor."

Sherri Jane, composed but worried that Bill might be too embarrassed to continue, leaned over her betrothed and whispered, "We don't need to finish the ceremony here. If you prefer, we can go to the minister's office, take care of the legalities, and send these people on to the reception."

"I'm okay," Bill said sheepishly, gathering himself back upon his feet.

The young minister quickly concluded the ceremony, rings were exchanged, and, following the obligatory kiss that concluded the vows, the couple was presented to the audience as husband and wife.

"By the authority vested in me as a minister," Robin Gage said, "I present to you Mr. and Mrs. William Edward Simons."

The chorale burst into triumphant lyrics written to Beethoven's "Ode to Joy," and the newlyweds beamed as they walked the center aisle to the rear of the auditorium.

The wedding reception was hosted at the Colonial Country Club, where the marriage proposal had occurred a year before. Bill and Sherri Jane, dancing with relatives and friends by the scores, were living a dream. With Major League baseball players at almost every table, the wedding reception was the number-one event on Fort Worth's high society calendar.

"When I tell Sherri Jane I've fallen for her, she'll know I'm telling her the truth," Bill said, teasing his bride as they greeted their guests in an endless line of well-wishers. Although embarrassed by his untimely fall during the wedding ceremony, Bill fielded questions and expressions of concern from the guests like a professional, which he certainly was. The celebration went late into the night, until the wedding party finally bid their *adieus* to their friends, driving off in Bill's brand new BMW roadster.

No one seemed to notice the run-down Dodge parked along the curbside a half block from the fashionable country club's main entrance, nor did anyone observe the pair of attentive eyes that had watched the parade of wedding guests who had attended the reception. After the wedding party's departure, the lurking watchman left his post, wiping away a few tears that had dropped onto his bearded cheeks.

The next day, photographs of the newlyweds were featured in newspapers from coast to coast. The wedding was front-page news in Fort Worth and San Antonio. *USA Today* did a spread on the couple in its "Life" section, revealing that the honeymoon destination was Kapalua Bay, Maui, Hawaii.

Chapter 12

Trouble in Paradise

"There is a generation that is pure in its own eyes, yet is not washed from its filthiness."

Proverbs 30:12

Randy was finishing some correspondence in his office when his personal assistant, Gwen Meaders, knocked lightly on his door.

"There's a gentleman here to see you," Gwen said, arching her eyebrows and cocking her head sideways. "Wouldn't give me his name but says it has something to do with Bill Simons."

"My luncheon begins in twenty minutes," Randy said, reminding Gwen of his scheduled appointment to attend the Texas Sports Hall of Fame's annual membership drive kick-off event. "Ask him to come in, but let him know I only have a couple of minutes."

Randy straightened his desk and picked up the morning newspaper lying on the floor, depositing it in the trash basket next to his favorite lounge chair. In less than four weeks, he would report with the coaches, pitchers, and catchers for early spring training drills.

The off-season gets shorter every year, he mused as he tidied up some files on his credenza. He was interrupted by a light rap on his door.

"Come in," he said, trying not to let his voice betray the bother he felt in having to entertain an unnamed, uninvited guest.

Slowly opening the door, a portly older man poked his head into Randy's office and asked, "Are you Randy Dobson?"

Randy noticed that the gentleman held an Eagles' baseball cap in his hand.

On the bright side, he must be one of our fans, Randy thought as he reached out to shake hands, saying, "Yes, I'm Randy Dobson. Have a seat. Did my assistant tell you I'm on my way to a luncheon and only have a couple of minutes?"

"Yes, she did," the man said quietly. "Thanks for seeing me. I only need a minute of your time. I'm Winston Simons, Bill's father."

Randy knew sketches of the story about Bill and his father, none of which suggested an amicable relationship. The last thing he needed was to be drawn into their longstanding feud.

"You may have heard that I have been estranged from Bill for almost twenty years. His mother and I couldn't make it with our marriage. It's one of those long stories, but the bottom line is that I messed up, and I regret every day that I was not there to see Bill grow up."

"It's a little late to do anything about that now," Randy said.

"Of course, I know that's right," Simons said, "but I just want Bill to know how deeply sorry I am that I wasn't there for him when he needed his father in his life. I want to ask for his forgiveness."

"Why have you come to me?" Randy asked.

Simons tucked his head, staring at the floor.

"Bill won't see me," he said. "I called on him one morning at his house, but he has such strong feelings about my abandoning him that he won't even talk to me."

"Mr. Simons, I'm truly sorry that you and Bill don't have a good relationship," Randy said empathetically. "When baseball season begins, I don't want any of my players stewing over family issues. If

I had my way, everyone would have a peaceful home life and lots of family members eager to support them at the ballpark."

Randy lowered his head, trying to sort through the man's simple request. He knew better than to get roped into someone else's dog fight; yet, if he could help his young pitcher come to peace with his past, it might be in everyone's best interest.

"No promises on my part," Randy said deliberately, "but if I have the right opportunity, I'll see if I can encourage Bill to sit down with you for a few minutes and allow you to offer him the olive branch."

"Thank you, Mr. Dobson," Simons said, standing and moving toward the door. "That's all I can ask. Thank you."

Randy followed him out, standing in the doorway as the old man shuffled down the hall toward the reception lobby.

This one won't be easy, he thought, grabbing his coat before leaving for his luncheon appointment.

* * * * *

On the same morning that Randy was listening to Mr. Simons, the manager's wife was also entertaining a visitor. Sherri Jane was back from Hawaii and had called Becky to see if she could drop by for a brief visit. Except for needing to spend a few minutes picking up groceries and stopping by the cleaners, Becky's day was wide open. She looked forward to hearing all about the newlyweds' trip to Maui.

A winter cold front had moved through Bexar County the night before, dropping temperatures into the high forties. Sherri Jane wore a white vest jacket, trimmed with a gray fox fur collar, over a burgundy turtleneck sweater and black worsted wool slacks. She was as glamorous as any movie star in Hollywood.

"Come in out of the cold," Becky said, giving Sherri Jane a warm hug to welcome her back home. "Tell me all about Maui. Randy and I want to go there sometime."

The two women sat next to one another on the living room sofa. Becky poured two cups of coffee, served with a small plate of glazed scones, placing them atop an oversized walnut-stained coffee table.

"You'd love Maui," Sherri Jane said, smiling. "It's like no other place I've been. We were there a week, but it was a long week." The smile was suddenly gone.

"What do you mean?" Becky asked.

"Becky," Sherri Jane said, sobbing and overcome with grief, "I don't know what to say. It was supposed to be an idyllic week in Hawaii, but it turned out to be the honeymoon from hell!"

Becky moved closer to Sherri Jane and put her arm around her shoulder as her sobs became louder and uncontrollable.

"Are you and Bill having problems?"

Unable to speak, Sherri Jane nodded her head.

The two women sat for several minutes, neither saying a word. Sherri Jane finally regained her composure, wiped away her tears with a tissue, and cleared her throat.

"Bill would be so angry if he knew I was here. He's hardly the same man I married four weeks ago. You cannot imagine how little things make him so angry…and mean."

Becky had heard Randy speak of Bill's temper on occasion but had dismissed it as being typical of many high-strung athletes who vented their frustrations through fits of anger. She could not imagine, however, that anyone could turn a honeymoon to Maui into a hellish experience.

"He *hit* me, Becky," Sherri Jane said, moaning as tears again slid down her cheeks. "He hit me."

"No!" Becky was incredulous. "What do you mean, *he hit you*?"

"Bill slapped me on the face…twice." Sherri Jane cried as if she were feeling the pain afresh. "We were having an argument about his dad and whether Bill should meet with him or not. I thought it might help them to iron out some things about their past, but I must have pressed the matter too far. The next thing I knew, he slapped me. When I pushed him away, he slapped me again. This is not what I thought marriage would be."

"You're right, Sherri Jane," Becky said. "All marriages have their ups and downs, a few good verbal fights thrown in to keep us honest with one another, but no woman should allow her husband to abuse her — verbally or physically."

"I'm afraid it's too late."

"No, not too late, but we must become proactive," Becky said. "I know a wonderful marriage counselor in Austin. Let me call and see if we can set an appointment. You need some professional help."

Becky spent the rest of the day with Sherri Jane. They drove to Fredericksburg, a unique Texas Hill Country town popular with tourists for its German food and Main Street shopping. After dining at the Peach Tree Inn, they shopped for kitchen accessories and linens and then took the back roads home, not arriving in San Antonio until early evening.

As Becky dropped Sherri Jane off in her driveway, she looked thoughtfully at the young wife.

"Sherri Jane, it will be all right."

Sherri Jane smiled in response, grateful to have someone to confide in, and nodded her head. For a moment, she believed Becky, but as she turned toward her front door, that optimism was snuffed out by a gust of cold winter wind.

Chapter 13

Digging Deep for Answers

"Incline your ear and hear the words of the wise, and apply your heart to my knowledge."

Proverbs 22:17

Sherri Jane made the hour-long trip from San Antonio to Austin, travelling north on I-35 in her Xian 250 coupe, one of many Chinese imports that had been flooding the United States market in recent years. Bill had surprised her at Christmas with the metallic silver roadster as his gift. He had spent an extra three thousand dollars to have bluebonnet blue leather seats and upholstery installed.

After returning from Hawaii, Bill had made a few syrupy-sweet overtures to Sherri Jane—usually when he needed something from her in return. He had not struck her again, but his verbal abuse was demeaning and occurred at the slightest provocation. Most recently, he had gone ballistic upon learning that Sherri Jane and Becky had had their girls' day out to Fredericksburg without his knowledge or approval.

Sherri Jane wanted what every young bride wanted in marriage: to be loved and to have someone to love; a mutual sense of place and of belonging to one another; and the security that comes from not feeling alone. She was certain that she loved Bill and believed that he felt the same toward her, but at the moment she needed guidance on how to set appropriate boundaries in order for their marital union to survive.

Upon hearing Becky's advice to get professional help, Sherri Jane had felt pangs of anxiety about seeing a counselor without telling Bill of the appointment. She had deliberately waited four weeks for Bill to leave for spring training in Arizona before making the call to the therapist's office. In her mind, it was just an exploratory visit, a chance to see if professional assistance would keep her marriage from taking off in a disastrous direction.

Exiting the interstate highway onto Martin Luther King Boulevard in Austin, Sherri Jane drove west toward the University of Texas campus, the massive buildings creating an imposing sight. She had visited the university on two other occasions, both when the TCU Horned Frogs were playing the Texas Longhorns in Saturday afternoon football games. It was hard for her to fathom how a university that once seemed huge with fifty thousand students could have grown to seventy-five thousand in the past ten years. The University of Texas, with its own U.S. Postal zip code, was indeed a city within a city.

The address card for Gerald H. Rusk, Ph.D., read 2104 North Lamar Avenue. A quick drive-by revealed the counselor's office was next to a bookstore in a small retail center with parking at the rear of the building. She found the lot, pulled her Xian coupe into a lined parking space, and walked nervously on a narrow sidewalk that led to Dr. Rusk's front door.

The reception room was small but furnished nicely with contemporary-style armchairs, tables, and lamps. Magazines, mostly medical journals and a few titles about family life, were arranged neatly on the blond coffee table. A middle-aged woman typing on a computer keyboard smiled at Sherri Jane as she entered the room.

"Good morning," the woman said in a warm, reassuring voice. "May I help you?"

"I have an appointment to see Dr. Rusk. My name is Sherri Jane Simons."

"Yes. Of course," the woman said, looking at her daily appointment book. "Dr. Rusk is expecting you. Please have a seat. May I offer you some coffee?"

"No, thank you," Sherri Jane said. She didn't need anything more to rattle her nerves this morning.

In less than a minute, a towering man in his early forties appeared at a door behind the receptionist's desk. Although the top of his head was completely bald, the psychologist wore a full beard that was well trimmed. He held a clipboard in his left hand and read the name on his file.

"Mrs. Simons?"

Dr. Rusk's office was much larger than the reception lobby. The therapist's desk and computer workstation were clustered at the back of the room, and stacks of bookshelves, filled with professional journals and scholarly tomes, covered three of the four walls. Four cushioned armchairs were arranged in a circle at the front of the office.

"Please, Mrs. Simons, have a seat," Dr. Rusk said, gesturing toward one of the chairs.

At the doctor's direction, Sherri Jane unfolded her story and shared her concerns about Bill and their marriage. Dr. Rusk, who taught marriage and family courses to undergraduates at the University of Texas, was a licensed marriage therapist. He listened attentively to Sherri Jane's story, taking a few notes, while reading gestures and every inflection in her voice. He had seen the symptoms before and knew her difficulties would not be easily overcome.

"Mrs. Simons," he said, "I will need several more sessions with you, and hopefully one or more with your husband in order to be certain of my findings, but it appears to me that you may be dealing with a spouse who suffers from a classic case of narcissism. Let me explain.

"Narcissistic Personality Disorder is a condition in which a person has an inflated sense of self-importance. Although we can't be sure what causes the problem, it often goes back to some issues in early childhood. The child may have had a traumatic experience with a parent or may not have been able to gain a parent's approval. The disorder usually begins to manifest itself when the child moves into early adulthood.

"You have already described to me many of the symptoms: reacting with rage when receiving personal criticism or when feeling a loss of control; preoccupation with personal success; demanding admiration or adulation from others; disregard for the feelings of others, often blaming them for his or her failures. I could go on, but you get the picture."

"Yes, I'm afraid I do," Sherri Jane said, dumbstruck by the similarities of these symptoms to the behavior she had seen lately in Bill.

"Please understand," Dr. Rusk said, "I am not saying that your husband has Narcissistic Personality Disorder. It would appear, however, from what you have told me this morning that we may be dealing with this issue or something very similar."

"What can be done to help us?" Sherri Jane asked. "I'm fearful that our marriage may be at risk. Is there something I need to change in order to help Bill work through his anger?"

"We all bring our own baggage into a marriage," Dr. Rusk said, "but truthfully, Mrs. Simons, there is little you can do to correct Bill's narcissistic behavior. My best advice is for you to refuse to become the victim of your husband's abuse, whether verbal or physical. That type of behavior is never acceptable. If he is open to visiting with me or another therapist who is qualified to counsel in these matters, encouraging him to do so would be the most helpful step you could possibly take."

"And what if he won't get help?" Sherri Jane asked. "What then?"

"Unfortunately, this type of conduct is not easily reversed without counseling, Mrs. Simons. I can't be sure about your husband, but if his behavior is consistent with most cases I've seen, he is likely to become more aggressive over time—not less."

Sherri Jane nodded, a look of fear embedded in her eyes. At the end of the hour, she reached down for her purse and made her way somberly toward the door, thanking Dr. Rusk for his counsel. She inserted the key into her car as though on autopilot and maneuvered out of the parking lot, pondering the past few weeks' events. As she eased on to the interstate, Sherri Jane turned on the Xian's satellite radio and listened to her favorite classical music station, allowing the intricate melodies to soothe her, transforming the drive from anxious and uncertain to near therapeutic. Nothing relieved her personal stress faster than listening to the lilting chords of an enchanting Viennese waltz. She replayed the words of Dr. Rusk over and over in her own mind, all of it to three-fourths time.

Chapter 14

A Championship Season

"A wise man fears and departs from evil, but a fool rages and is self-confident."
Proverbs 14:16

Bill had been gone three weeks, attending the Eagles' spring training camp, before Sherri Jane boarded a Southwest Airlines flight in San Antonio and joined him and his teammates in Peoria, Arizona. Becky met her at the Phoenix Sky Harbor International Airport, chauffeuring her to the residential subdivision where many of the players and their families were staying.

"Well, tell me! How did you get along with Dr. Rusk?" Becky asked, hoping her referral had been helpful to her young friend.

"He's brilliant," Sherri Jane said. "He seems to know exactly what I'm feeling, and I know he understands what Bill and I have been experiencing in our marriage. Dr. Rusk thinks Bill's anger may be a symptom of deep-seated narcissism. He says that celebrities are especially vulnerable because they thrive on public adulation. They're so used to getting their way that even simple conflicts with a spouse will upset them and trigger explosive anger, like a kid throwing a temper tantrum because he doesn't get what he wants."

"Is it treatable?" Becky asked.

"It can be, but I'm going to need Bill's participation in the therapy," Sherri Jane said, sighing. "I'm not sure how he'll react when I tell him I've seen Dr. Rusk three times since he left for spring training."

Becky helped Sherri Jane carry her luggage inside a modest two-bedroom patio home, within easy driving distance from the Eagles' training facilities. Bill was expecting her arrival, but he was at an exhibition game in Mesa and would not be home until early evening. Upon entering the bedroom, Sherri Jane saw a handwritten note lying on the neatly made bed. It was from Bill. She picked it up and read silently, brushing a tear from her eyes.

My dearest Sherri Jane,

These have been three of the longest weeks in my life. I have missed you and everything about you. You make my life complete in every possible way. I love you.

Bill

Sherri Jane, choked with emotion, passed the note to Becky, who quickly scanned Bill's message.

"That's so sweet. Everything's going to work out," Becky said reassuringly.

The women embraced, said their goodbyes, and Becky went on her way. Sherri Jane unpacked her suitcases, settling into her temporary living quarters. Her plan was to stay two weeks in Arizona. That would be within a day of when the Eagles would break camp and head back home, playing their last few exhibition games in Albuquerque, Arlington, and Houston, before meeting the New Orleans Gators on Opening Day at Gainsworth Stadium.

When Bill arrived home, he swept Sherri Jane off her feet, showering her with kisses in the same way he had done when they were dating.

"Look at you, gorgeous," Bill said, beaming. "You are tonic for a weary man's soul."

Bill's enthusiastic welcome was exactly what Sherri Jane had hoped it would be. He appeared to be so genuine in his expression of affection.

Maybe I was premature in seeking professional help.

Not wanting to spoil the joy of their blissful reunion, Sherri Jane made no mention to Bill of her visits with Dr. Rusk. She had intended to introduce the delicate subject of marriage counseling the next morning at breakfast, but after seeing how excited Bill was to see her, she let the matter drop the entire two weeks they were in Arizona.

* * * * *

From the moment the Eagles set foot on the lush grass at Gainsworth Stadium, a new attitude permeated the team. This was San Antonio's year—"The Year of the Eagles," as their public relations office ballyhooed in the team's yearbook and press releases. It was a winning attitude, and the team played according to script, with one outstanding performance after another on the baseball diamond. Once again, the Eagles were off to a fast start, leading the National League South by nine games at the All-Star break.

Bill Simons was having a career year, losing only one game before going into the mid-season break. Not only had he been named to the All-Star team, he had been designated to start for the National League team when they met the American League's best at Dodgers' Stadium in Los Angeles. At an early age, Bill had become one of the premier pitchers in Major League Baseball.

Sherri Jane continued to keep the issue of counseling to herself. She and Bill were managing the marriage as well as they possibly could under the circumstances. They were together when the Eagles were playing in San Antonio, and she accompanied him on a few of the road trips to cities she enjoyed visiting: New Orleans, New York, and Los Angeles. They had weathered a few spats, one or two heated arguments, but no slaps or physical threats had occurred. She had decided to roll the dice, taking her chances that the relationship would get better over time.

With her parents living near Ventura, Sherri Jane scheduled a flight to the West Coast to attend the All-Star game with her mom and dad. She stayed with Bill and the other All-Stars at a posh hotel near Dodgers' Stadium but spent the greater part of two days visiting with her parents, careful not to mention any problems she was having with her marriage. Walton Laird had four seats in an executive suite reserved exclusively for Dodger front office personnel and insisted that his daughter join him and her mother for the big game.

The pregame ceremonies completed and the National Anthem having been performed by Rickety Sticks, the nation's hottest rock band sensation, it was time for the contest to begin. Bill stood on the mound in his San Antonio Eagles home uniform, white with silver-and-blue trim, ready to throw the game's first pitch. Sherri Jane sat anxiously on the edge of her seat. At this moment, she was especially proud to be Mrs. Bill Simons.

Bill looked in for his sign from Roy Medley, the Chicago Cubs catcher and one of the best defensive players in the game. The Eagles' ace went into his familiar windup and let the first pitch fly toward home plate, where Juan Pedro, centerfielder for the Oakland A's, was waiting in the batter's box. The stadium's radar gun displayed the fastball's speed at ninety-six miles per hour. What it didn't calibrate was the speed of the ball as it came off Pedro's bat, but everyone in the stands could tell that when it finally landed, it had gone more than 414 feet over the left-centerfield wall. It was a stunning way to begin the ballgame, and for the National League, it was all downhill from there.

Bill lasted two-thirds of an inning, giving up six base hits and four earned runs. He could not hide his displeasure at being removed from the game so early. A few hecklers sitting in the front rows of the field boxes made matters worse, booing and jeering as Bill entered the dugout. He slammed his glove on the bench, walked to the water cooler, and promptly pushed it over on its side.

When Randy Dobson, who was serving as one of the coaches for the National League team, grabbed Bill to settle him down, the angry hurler shoved his manager aside, yelling, "Get out of my way! I don't need your lectures on how I'm supposed to behave."

Pausing for a second, Bill turned to Randy, looking him directly in the eye, and said, "And tell your wife to keep away from Sherri Jane. We don't need either one of you meddling in our marriage." The whole incident was caught on television cameras and broadcasted coast-to-coast on ESPN.

Although Bill's outburst in Los Angeles resulted in major repercussions with the Eagles' baseball team, especially its management and front office, it did not keep the team from performing well on the field. After the All-Star break, the Eagles finished the season as mightily as they had begun, winning the National League South by thirteen games over the second-place Atlanta Braves. This time, however, they walked through the playoffs, routing the Pittsburgh Pirates in divisional play and sweeping the San Francisco Giants to win the National League pennant.

The last hurdle of the year was the sweetest of all. The San Antonio Eagles beat the New York Yankees, four games to two, to become baseball's World Champions. Bill Simons won the Cy Young Award for being the league's best pitcher, posting a record of thirty wins and five losses. He was the first thirty-game winner in Major League Baseball since Detroit's Denny McLain accomplished the feat with thirty-one victories in 1968.

The Eagles' post-season celebration was good for the whole organization. President Ohlmstead invited the team to the White House; Randy was named National League Manager of the Year; and Bill was on the cover of every baseball journal in America. The young pitcher from Kansas had become a nationally acclaimed baseball icon—more fodder to fuel the young star's inflated ego.

Chapter 15

Killing Daddy

"Wine is a mocker, strong drink is a brawler, and whoever is led astray by it is not wise."

Proverbs 20:1

Bill Simons wasted little time in making his demands known to management. He was the indisputable hero of the San Antonio Eagles, who had completed their most successful season in franchise history. Now, Bill was insisting that the organization renegotiate his contract to reflect the enhanced value he brought to the team.

Currently receiving $3 million per year, Bill demanded a five-year extension of his contract at an annual salary of $18 million. His agent had presented a formal request to management, asking that the matter be settled before the opening of February's spring training. Wil Laird and the owners, although knowing Bill was worth this type of money, were balking at the enormous increase being sought by their superstar.

"Where does he come up with a figure like that?" Eugene Gainsworth asked at the impromptu breakfast meeting of the Eagles' owners and upper management.

"It's in line with the salary Milwaukee paid Jorgensen last year," Laird said, "but Jorgie has spent fifteen years in the Majors. This kid's been up three years and thinks he owns the place. I don't get it."

"What if we shop him on the trade market?" Louise Jones, the most recent addition to the owners' circle, asked. She was the heiress to her father's brewery fortune and relished her new role with the Eagles. "His trade value must have soared this past season, and we can let someone else worry about renegotiating his contract."

"Randy, we haven't heard from you," Gainsworth said. "What's your thought on the matter?"

Randy had been invited to attend the owners' meeting in order to add perspective from his position as field manager. He grimaced at Ms. Jones' suggestion of trading Bill. This one player had carried the team on his shoulders throughout the year, and if the Eagles had any hope of repeating as World Champions, they would need Bill at the top of their pitching rotation again next year.

"I understand the dilemma you face," Randy said. "Ninety million dollars over five years represents a healthy slice out of your television revenue and a ton of ticket sales. If every young player had the same grandiose ideas about his worth to this club, there wouldn't be enough money in all of Texas to underwrite your payroll.

"At the same time, Bill is no ordinary player. Last year he established himself as one of baseball's true superstars. Thirty-nine other teams wish they had a Bill Simons on their roster. If the Eagles want to compete, we need to find a way to keep him in the fold."

"What about his behavior off the field?" Gainsworth asked. "That incident at the All-Star game was reprehensible. If you ask me, he's an embarrassment to his teammates and to this organization."

"If you knew the stories Walton has told me about the way Bill treats Sherri Jane, you wouldn't be so proud to have him on this team," Laird said. "When I was manager, I wouldn't have put up with him."

"With all respect, Wil, if you would have had any pitcher half as good as Bill Simons, you might have won a pennant," Randy said, trying to stand up for his player without being disrespectful to his venerable colleague. "I'm here to tell you that I, for one, believe we need to find a way to work through this contract negotiation and keep Bill Simons in an Eagle uniform."

The discussion continued for another hour until Gainsworth suggested the owners take a vote to see where they stood. By a show of hands, they voted three to two to pay Bill the increased salary and extend the contract for five years. Randy took a deep sigh of relief, thanked the owners, and excused himself from the meeting.

Upon returning to his office, Randy found the Eagles' hitting coach, Gabby Rhodes, seated in the manager's lounge chair.

"How'd it go?" Gabby asked. "Did the owners listen?"

"They listened," Randy said assuredly. "Bill's going to be with the Eagles for another five years."

"He's a terror on wheels," Gabby said, smiling, "but he's our terror, right?"

"Right," Randy said.

"By the way," Gabby said, reaching into his pocket for a small newspaper clipping, "have you seen this?"

Randy took the paper from Gabby and read a two-column article that appeared in the morning edition of the *Express-News*. The headline read *Simons' Father Found Dead*.

Randy quickly scanned the article, reading that the elder Simons had apparently taken an overdose of sleeping pills. He was found by a housekeeper in an Amarillo motel.

"Come on, Gabby," Randy said. "We need to find Bill and make sure he's handling this all right. The last time I tried to encourage him to visit his dad, he almost bit my head off."

The two men hustled out to the parking lot, where they took Gabby's Jeep, affectionately known by Eagles players as the "team limo," and sped to the north side of town. Bill and Sherri Jane had recently purchased a house within a mile of La Canterra Country Club. Weaving in and out of traffic along Interstate-10, Gabby exited the highway and turned into a new subdivision, filled with newly constructed million-dollar houses. Once they were in the neighborhood, Randy guided him to the Simons'

Mediterranean-style home, tucked away on a tree-lined cul-de-sac.

Sherri Jane answered the door.

"Come in. I thought you might drop by. Bill's out on the patio. He's been drinking all morning. I can't be sure whether he's mourning or celebrating."

"How did he learn about it?" Gabby asked.

"A deputy sheriff came by last night. He brought a few personal belongings that were found in the motel room, along with a note addressed to Bill, but he doesn't want to read it. He snapped at me when I suggested he open the envelope. Come on back. Can I get you something to drink?"

"Thanks, Sherri Jane. We're fine," Randy said as he and Gabby followed her into the kitchen and on to the outside door that led to the patio.

Randy and Gabby found Bill sprawled on an overstuffed lounge chair near a shimmering blue swimming pool surrounded by a meticulously landscaped lawn. On an Indian summer November morning, he wore golfing shorts, a green-and-white polo shirt, and a pair of Birkenstock sandals. Sunglasses hid his bleary eyes, reddened by spending the last two hours nursing a bottle of Grey Goose Vodka.

"Sorry about your dad," Randy said, opening the conversation.

"What's to be sorry about?" Bill asked sarcastically.

"You know, we've had this discussion before, Bill," Randy said. "We just have one father in this world, and when he's gone, there's bound to be a sense of loss. I'm sorry for you."

"That's how you feel about it, but not me," Bill said. "On the baseball diamond, you can tell me how to think, but when it comes to something like this—you know, family issues—I'll do the thinking for myself."

"Bill, the owners met this morning, and I'm proud of the position they're taking on your contract. You should be hearing from them this afternoon, but I think you'll be pleased with their decision."

"I'm glad you're going to be back, kid," Gabby said. "We'll have another good year."

It was clear that Bill was in no mood for conversation, and so the visitors bid him and Sherri Jane goodbye.

"Why's Bill so disrespectful of you?" Gabby asked, steering the Jeep unconsciously to the stadium. "From what I know about his situation, you're the best advocate he has with the owners and the front office."

"Have you ever heard of the 'killing daddy syndrome,' Gabby?" Bill asked.

"I guess not."

"Some young adults, especially men, have a hard time dealing with their elders," Randy said. "They compete with the generation ahead of them, advancing themselves by making the older generation look inept or out of touch. The shrinks call it 'killing daddy.' It just means these messed-up kids see the older generation as a threat to their own senses of self-importance. Doesn't that sound like Bill?"

"Makes no sense to me," Gabby said. "What a sorry way to live life, always making yourself look good at someone else's expense."

"Especially when he has everything in the world going for him," Randy said. "When you're as successful as he is, there's no need to demean someone else, but I think he's warped that way, and from some things you just can't come back."

Chapter 16

Hiring a New Manager

*"Do you see a man wise in his own eyes?
There is more hope for a fool than for him."*
Proverbs 26:12

Bill awoke from a restless slumber. Bits and pieces of his nocturnal visions raced through his mind like colored jewels seen through a kaleidoscope. Whenever his father appeared in one of his dreams, he spent a wasted night in bed.

Over and over Bill replayed trailers from his days in San Antonio: stepping onto the lush, green turf at Gainsworth Stadium for the first time; dazzling Major League hitters with his awesome cutter; throwing a no-hitter against the Mets. The question of the hour was whether he would be given the opportunity to experience the wonder of it all again, this time as the Eagles' manager.

Remembering that Randy had promised to call after visiting with Eugene Gainsworth, Bill picked up his cell phone and pushed Speed Dial 2, the number Randy had worn on his baseball uniform. After four rings, Bill disconnected the call, preferring not to leave a message. What he wanted to tell his former manager needed to be said in person, not through voicemail.

Bill's feelings toward Randy had deteriorated in recent years. There was a time when he believed his mentor would do just about anything he asked of him, but in recent years a barrier had come between the two men. Intuitively, he believed Sherri Jane had much to do with the current situation. Randy and Becky had digested a steady diet of "Bill bashing" when Sherri Jane had divorced him and moved to Los Angeles a little over ten years ago.

What was it about Sherri Jane that everyone believed her?

Their marriage had been a rocky venture, surviving ten years of blows and counterblows, but Bill refused to believe the lies his former wife told about him and his boorish behavior as a husband. The way he saw it, she was neurotic, always finding fault with his conduct or demeanor.

She was impossible to please.

The marriage had not borne any children, and for that Bill was grateful. A career in baseball was not the ideal situation for a single father with custody rights to a household of teenagers. Bill knew in his heart that any judge would have awarded him custody of their children, had there been any.

Sherri Jane would have been an unfit mother, incapable of caring for any children. She could hardly take care of herself, always running off to Becky for advice, let alone kids.

Thankfully, he never had to fight that battle.

The divorce itself was a messy affair, scandalized in the tabloids and featured nightly on celebrity news channels. Before filing, Sherri Jane had sought an injunction for protection against domestic violence. Bill had become belligerent in the home, pushing and swatting at Sherri Jane as if she were a punching bag in the gym. Two San Antonio police officers forcibly removed him from his own house, and the judge prohibited Bill from having direct contact with Sherri Jane. Three weeks later, she filed a petition in Bexar County for divorce.

As he poured a cup of freshly brewed coffee, Bill tried to think more about his future than his past. If prudent minds prevailed, the opportunity to manage the San Antonio Eagles was well within his grasp. He had been an unqualified success as a player in the Major Leagues, and with three winning seasons of managing at Triple-A Austin, Bill felt good about his probabilities. Given the chance, he was confident that he would enjoy similar success as a manager in the big leagues.

While sipping a second cup of coffee and reading the morning sports section of the *San Antonio Express-News*, Bill heard his cell phone ringing in the bedroom. He walked quickly from his breakfast table toward the master bedroom suite, finding his phone on top of his dresser.

"Hello," Bill said, trying to catch his breath.

"Mr. Simons, this is Ann Everett in Mr. Eugene Gainsworth's office. I have been asked to call you to see if you will be available for an interview with the owners of the San Antonio Eagles. They would like to see you next Monday at two o'clock in Mr. Gainsworth's office. Is that time suitable with you?"

"Yes, of course," Bill answered cheerfully. This was the call he had been waiting for. *Maybe Randy did some good after all.*

Hiring a New Manager

No sooner than Bill had finished the call from Ms. Everett than his home phone began to ring. From the caller-ID, he could see the call was from Randy.

"Hello," Bill said, his voice monotone, as if the call were from a complete stranger.

"Hi, Bill."

"Oh, Randy, it's you," Bill said, feigning surprise.

"Listen, Bill, I just talked with Eugene, and I think you'll be getting a call to interview for the job," Randy said. "Just thought I'd give you a heads up."

"You're three minutes late," Bill said chidingly. "I just got a call asking me to appear for an interview next Monday. I think this deal is coming to a head."

"Great, Bill," Randy said, pleased that the message had already been relayed. "Have you heard that the owners are planning to interview Owen Williams as well?"

Williams was the current manager of the San Diego Padres.

Bill was stunned for a moment, silent as Randy's arrow sunk in. It almost sounded as if Randy was pleased to be the bearer of bad news of a significant rival for the position.

"No, I hadn't heard about Owen," Bill said. "How serious are they about looking at him for the job?"

"Serious enough to interview him," Randy said. "Again, I have to tell you that my influence is practically nil in the decision. Eugene wants me to stay out of the owners' way, and I intend to do that. I've done what I promised with Eugene. The rest is up to you. Good luck."

* * * * *

Three weeks had lapsed since the Eagles' owners and front office personnel had interviewed Bill Simons and Owen Williams, both legitimate candidates for the team's managerial vacancy. The interviews had been constructive. Both men had impressive credentials, and each had expressed his willingness to accept the job if tendered to him. Now the decision lay in the hands of the owners.

Eugene Gainsworth called another meeting of the owners, this time asking that they convene at ten o'clock in the boardroom in Gainsworth Tower. All five of the owners were present, none wanting to miss the opportunity to select the next manager for their beloved Eagles. Wil Laird and his top aides were also invited, but he had recused himself because of family ties to Sherri Jane.

"Let's call this meeting to order," Gainsworth said, bellowing in much the same manner with which he was accustomed in running his oil company. "We have only one item on the agenda today. When this meeting is over, the Eagles will have a new field manager."

"Owen has far more experience as a Major League manager," said Robert Faykus, a prominent attorney who owned ten percent of the franchise. "From what I have heard, Owen is a players' manager, always going the second mile for his team. He has my vote."

Linda Romero, whose mother, Louise Jones, had been an active participant in the owners' circle until she suffered a fatal stroke three years earlier, was a big fan of Bill Simons. She had grown up watching Bill pitch in Gainsworth Stadium and chose to believe only the best about him.

"I don't understand how we could possibly turn our back on Bill Simons," Linda said. "For twenty years he has been loyal to the Eagles, both as a player and as our Triple-A manager in Austin. How can we deny him the opportunity to manage this team?"

"If you had been sitting in this chair as long as I have, Ms. Ramirez, you—"

"It's Romero, Mr. Gainsworth. Romero!"

"Excuse me, but whatever," Gainsworth said, "if you'd sat around this table as I have for the past twenty-plus years, you would think twice before taking on all the trauma Bill Simons will bring to the position. I don't trust him."

Stuart Ross, chairman and chief executive officer of USAA, one of the nation's largest financial companies and one of the most respected business enterprises headquartered in San Antonio, cleared his throat to speak.

"I like Bill Simons too. Our company has used him on many occasions to speak and appear at business functions. He has always acquitted himself as a gentleman in my presence. And, as Linda has observed, he is well known to our city and to our fans.

"However, I find it hard to ignore the proven track record of Owen Williams. He enjoys a good reputation as a baseball man and as a decent human being. Unfortunately, Bill has made some enemies along the way. I don't want to see the Eagles sullied by his indiscretions in the past or those he might incur in the future. I'm afraid I must cast my vote for Owen."

The only shareholder who had not spoken on the subject was Daniel G. Tinsley, a major partner in a regional accounting firm. Tinsley was known for his meticulous scrutiny of the team's financial records.

"I confess that I don't know much about Owen Williams," Tinsley said when Gainsworth asked him for his opinion. "What I do know is that the Falcons have had winning seasons in Austin the past three years, but at a fairly steep cost to the Eagles' organization. Simons has consistently overspent his budget, accumulating a sizeable deficit. He gives our own front office fits with his temper tantrums, and I have it from a good source that he has been trying to get a group of Houston businessmen who are closely connected with the Astros to buy out our Triple-A club so that he can change the affiliation. He doesn't appear to be ideally suited for the job we have to offer."

Discussion around the board table continued for two-and-a-half hours. When the comments became repetitive and irrelevant, Gainsworth called for a vote. Although it was fairly obvious how each owner felt about the candidates, a secret ballot was used, and it was weighted according to the percentage of ownership each voter had in the franchise. By a vote of four to one, representing eighty-five percent of the club's ownership, Owen Williams was named the new manager of the San Antonio Eagles. Eugene Gainsworth made a hasty call, breaking the news to his friend Randy Dobson.

Chapter 17

Unsettled Business

> "There is a way that seems right to a man,
> but its end is the way of death."
>
> **Proverbs 16:25**

The front page of the *Express-News* and three pages of its sports section were filled with the press release and related stories about Owen Williams' appointment as the new field manager of the San Antonio Eagles. Having flown to Texas immediately following the owners' decision, Williams, donning an Eagles cap and jersey, and Eugene Gainsworth were featured in a color photograph that dominated the newspaper's front page.

Bill read the article with complete disgust. Late yesterday afternoon, he had received a telephone call from Gainsworth himself informing him of the owners' decision.

He didn't have the decency to come tell me in person, Bill thought as he slammed down the receiver. The news had sent him into a drunken rage that lasted well into the night, and now he was reminded about it all over again.

Making matters worse, Butch Lemery, the most widely read baseball journalist in Texas, had written a side-bar piece explaining all the reasons Bill Simons had not been selected for the vacant position.

They had the gall to carry that picture, Bill murmured, glaring at the image of him shoving Randy in the dugout at the infamous All-Star game. *That was almost twenty years ago. Will they never let that go? Leo Durocher, Billy Martin, Earl Weaver, Lou Piniella—they all got away with temper tantrums as managers; why do they hold my outbursts against me?*

Bill cringed as he read the remarks attributed to owner Daniel G. Tinsley.

What is all this garbage about deficits in Austin? My job is to win baseball games; their job is to cover the costs. And this silly idea that I was selling out to Houston? That was just a private conversation of what-ifs. I never meant anything by it. What is Tinsley thinking?

Then Bill discovered the shocker. On the front page of the sports section was a "grip-and-grin" photograph of Randy Dobson and Wil Laird.

Look at them, smiling like rattlesnakes foraging for field mice.

In addition to the news about Williams, the Eagles had announced that Randy would succeed Laird as general manager of the team.

That's what this is all about! All this time he's been professing his neutrality. I'll bet he's been orchestrating the move through Gainsworth from the very beginning. I hate him! I hate him!

As he stewed over the story lines and the various individuals involved, Bill began to see what he thought was a conspiracy, with Gainsworth, Wil Laird, and Dobson at the helm.

The good ole boys!

He tried to connect the dots.

Gainsworth treats Randy like a son. Laird is Sherri Jane's uncle, and he has spread vicious lies to Gainsworth about me. Randy wants the general manager's job and doesn't want to risk upsetting Gainsworth or Laird by supporting me to become the Eagles' new manager. Consequently, the only way Randy can become general manager is to get rid of me. That's it! This entire charade has been a conspiracy enabling Randy to work a few more years for the Eagles!

Bill had hit the liquor cabinet hard the night before, but now, at ten o'clock in the morning, he chose to bring out the big bottles once again. Craving something to dull the pain, he took one shot of whiskey, straight, and then another.

This is not right! It's just not right!

The alcohol gave him no comfort, nor did it calm his wrath. Finding his favorite lounge chair, he fell into its deep leather seat and turned on the television. The news anchors at ESPN's Sports Central were reporting the announcements about Williams and Dobson. Footage from yesterday's press conference began to play.

They were all there: Gainsworth, Laird, Williams, and Dobson.

Dobson. What a snake in the grass.

Bill turned the television off and stumbled to the master bedroom closet. He fumbled through sweaters and until his hand struck the cool metal of his Glock 37. He grabbed the automatic pistol, along with a ten-round magazine of cartridges, and headed for the garage.

If I can't work for the Eagles, neither can he!

A cold front was working its way through the Texas Hill Country, leaving the roads damp from a light, but steady mist. Bill felt the chill as he opened the automatic garage door and slid into his black BMW 760Li sedan. Laying the Glock next to him on the front seat, he backed out of the garage, threw the car into drive, and stomped on the accelerator, instantly sending the 535-horsepower vehicle out of the driveway and on to the rain-soaked streets.

For the next few minutes, as Bill sped across the 1604 Loop west toward I-10, he engaged in a one-man pep rally, shouting epithets and expletives directed toward all who had been part of the great conspiracy to ruin his good name. He was a victim of their maniacal manipulation, all centered on destroying him and everything he had achieved in his life.

Randy is just like my father. He has never thought of my well-being. Everything is always about him. He's used me. He's lied to me. All that Randy has ever wanted is what's good for Randy. Why did I listen to him? Why did I trust him?

Honk! Honk! Bill pressed hard on the BMW's horn as he wove in and around the cautious traffic.

How could Gainsworth and his cronies turn their backs on me? After all I have done to pad their pocketbooks? It's not fair. Justice has not prevailed in his case. Sometimes a guy has to help the cause of justice along.

He turned north on I-10 West and unleashed the powerful BMW sedan. Fourteen miles to Boerne.

* * * * *

Traffic had stacked up for three miles on the interstate north of San Antonio. Randy was in no hurry, returning home from a breakfast appointment with Owen Williams and Wil Laird. The men had spent a couple of hours preparing for the transition of leadership: Laird to Dobson, Dobson to Williams. The meeting was amicable and productive. Laird was glad to step out of baseball after many years as player, manager, and general manager. Randy was equally pleased to leave his position to someone who had unbridled passion to achieve mountaintop experiences as a field manager.

With traffic at a standstill, weary drivers began wondering what had caused the highway to become a virtual parking lot. Randy turned on his radio, hoping for some road report that would shed light on what lay ahead. He had heard sirens ten minutes ago, but all was quiet now. Finally, vehicles began to move again, creeping along at a snail's pace.

Coming over the crest of a hill, Randy saw the flashing lights of patrol cars, ambulances, and wreckers, all converged on one spot of the interstate highway. An officer was directing traffic toward the right lane and shoulder to avoid the massive collision that had occurred in the left lane, near the median. An eighteen-wheeler and a black car of an undetermined make and model were practically welded together in an ugly heap of metal and debris. It was obvious to Randy and to all who passed the scene that someone had lost their life in the collision. It never occurred to him that the auto fatality was Bill Simons.

The next morning Randy read every article written about Bill Simons in the local and national newspapers. Most accentuated the positive, leaving unsaid, for the moment, the darker side of Bill's personality. What had occurred was reported as a tragic accident on a slippery highway; it could have happened to anyone.

"Did you see they found a gun in the car?" Becky asked as she refilled Randy's cup of coffee.

"Yes, I did. I wonder what that was all about."

"He wasn't stable, Randy. I didn't trust him. Did you?"

"Trust? No. But I never thought of him being a threat to anyone except himself. His life could be written as a Greek tragedy—so much talent and opportunity left unfulfilled."

* * * * *

A memorial service was held for Bill at the Liberal High School Gymnasium, where a standing-room-only crowd gathered to say goodbye to the town's most famous native son. The local mayor spoke, as did Bill's former high school baseball coach and the pastor of the Baptist church. Each extolled the fallen Eagle as an honorable hero, worthy of the esteem in which he was held by his boyhood community.

At the graveside service, Randy and Becky stood next to Sherri Jane Fisher, who had made the trip from California to pay her respects to the first man she had ever loved. She wiped tears from her cheeks as the pastor read from the Scriptures and led a final prayer.

Following her divorce, Sherri Jane had worked for a public relations firm in Santa Monica. Two years later, she had married Jackson J. Fisher, Jr., an attorney who was senior partner in a Los Angeles law firm. Sherri Jane had met Fisher when her father had engaged the firm to assist with his estate planning. Reluctant to reenter the dating scene, Sherri Jane rebuffed the persistent attorney's advances for a few months, but with help from her personal counselor she had come to believe that not all men were cut from the same cloth as Bill Simons. The Fishers had two daughters, both of whom had chosen not to attend the funeral, instead remaining in California with their father.

"Are you happy, Sherri Jane?" Randy asked, placing his arm around her shoulder.

"Very happy," she answered. "You and Becky were my lifesavers during those tough years in San Antonio, but by the grace of God, I'm on the other side of that ordeal. I'm deeply saddened by Bill's tragic death, but it can't take away anything from the family I enjoy now. Jackson is so good to me, and we both adore the girls. Yes, I'm happy."

"He who troubles his own house will inherit the wind, and the fool will be the servant to the wise of heart."
Proverbs 11:29

Additional Titles
by the Author

J. Terry Johnson, a native of Springfield, Missouri, retired from Oklahoma Christian University in 2000 after a thirty-two-year tenure with the Oklahoma City liberal arts university. From 1974 until 1995, Johnson was president and chief executive officer; he served an additional five years as the university's chancellor. In 2000, Johnson was inducted into the Oklahoma Higher Education Hall of Fame. He currently lives in Horseshoe Bay, Texas.

Since his retirement, Johnson has authored nine books, all of which can be purchased at www.Amazon.com, www.BarnesandNoble.com, or from the author at Johnson Books, P.O. Box 8106, Horseshoe Bay, TX 78657.

Jubilee: A colorful pictorial history of the first fifty years of Oklahoma Christian University. (2000)

Fairways and Green Pastures: A coffee table gift book offering an inspirational walk through each hole of Ram Rock Golf Course at the Horseshoe Bay Resort. (Foreword by Byron Nelson; 2006)

Cardinal Fever (Foreword by Whitey Herzog; 2009); ***Kirby*** (Foreword by John Ashcroft; 2008); ***Awakenings*** (Foreword by Pat Boone; 2010): A trilogy of memoirs about a boy growing up in the Missouri Ozarks.

Two Parts Sunshine: A combined biography and cookbook from the life of Marty Johnson, the author's wife. (Foreword by Sherri Coale; 2010)

10 Critical Factors in Fundraising: A digest covering the essential elements of raising financial support for nonprofit organizations. (Foreword by Andrew K. Benton; 2011)

Be of Good Cheer: A daily devotional to encourage the reader's spiritual growth. (2012)

Wounded Eagle: A novel about an imaginary Major League Baseball team in San Antonio, Texas. (Foreword by Nolan Ryan; 2013)